Love Me With Tenderness

Ewart F. Brown

Your Town Press

Edited by:
Janet L. Williams.

Designed by:
Ewart Brown
Janet Williams

Printed in the United States of America by
Your Town Press
2773 Cherry Ave. N.E.
Salem OR 97303

Library of Congress-in-Publication Data

Brown, Ewart
Love me with tenderness

ISBN 0-976 3347-0-4

Chapter Thoughts

Dedication

This book
is dedicated to my dear mother
Ruby Jane Brown
now deceased
who lovingly sacrificed much
to ensure for me a future
for which I am ever
thankful.

She often said to me,
"The one who talks to you about others,
will later talk to others about you."
I carry this thought with me still.

Acknowledgment

Thanks to my wife Lynn for her understanding and support. Many hours have been spent at home busy writing and away working on this project. Her patience was comforting and her input very valuable.

Thanks to Gary Parks, my partner in ministry, who has a passion for resolving conflicts the right way and who encourages me to apply the biblical method towards solving conflicts.

Thanks to Janet Williams for the many hours she spent on this book as reader and editor. She also contributed to the organization and formatting and was extremely helpful in catching awkward language structures.

Thanks to Gary Williams for his support during the times his wife Janet was working on this project.

Thanks to Ulani Alynn Brown, my granddaughter, for posing for the pictures on the front and back covers.

Pictures by Kellie Lusk
Blue Frog Graphics
Battle Ground, Washington

Purpose of Writing –

The Christian community is God's gift to the universe. All of us who accept the name "Christian" belong to this community or family. This means that we are close. We are connected and we care for one another. We cry, laugh, and hope together. But unfortunately, there are times when unfamily-like behaviors steal into our circle and we hurt our family intentionally or unintentionally causing tears and brokenness. How sad. I have received some of these unfamily-like behaviors. They hurt for years, even after I have forgiven the individuals.

When a wound is made, it heals, but leaves a scar. And the humanness of us find it hard to deal with it. We wish it was not there. You and I have observed others being beaten by these unfamily-like behaviors. And we say, "I am glad that was not me." But why should anyone suffer such mental beating from someone who loves us? Why do we experience so much pain caused by our Christian family?

Recently I was at a church meeting, not the church in which I am presently serving. It soon became clear that this was not going to be a Christ-like, warm, and friendly meeting. The family members were going to tear each other apart. It soon began and the pain was flying thickly through the air. A few individuals attempted to save the moment from emotional destruction, but those who had come to fight and destroy were immovable. And I asked myself the question, "How could we be so heartless towards our fellow Christians? Do we not understand how it feels when we are hurt?" If you have never been hurt, may you never. Please know that I do know how it feels. I have been there.

Following the meeting, I went home and was troubled during the night. Early the next morning, 3 a.m., I was awakened and had a strong urge to write about how Christians are to love. The content of this book that you are about to experience then began to flow into my mind.

A Message to My Reader –

Dear Friend, I am reaching out to you in this book, to allow our hearts to talk. And from this our time together, hopefully, our Christian family and our world will be a better and safer place in which to live. You and I can make that difference. We cannot change another person, but we can choose to change. I can change me, through God's help. Can we agree that, today and tomorrow, we will be kind to others no matter how we are treated? We learn to love others by understanding God's love for us. So then, can we agree that by the love of Jesus, we will ***Love with Tenderness***, as Jesus loves us?

The Journey –

Surely, our time together will take us to painful memories, even though no one enjoys visiting Pain Lane. But we will also visit pleasurable memories. Wherever I take you, I know that you also have been there. Let us pray for God to walk with us on this journey. Our walk may make a difference for tomorrow and eternity.

Understanding Love –

In the beginning of my Christian journey, others told me that God and Jesus loved me. At the age of twelve, it was not clear to me how God and Jesus loved me and how I could love them in return, since I could not see them. But as I grew in the spiritual walk, it became easier to understand God's love and consequently easier to love God in return. It is true, loving God and Jesus is different from loving my family or a friend.

In recent time, God and Jesus have been communicating to me through the written word and through my mind how much they love me. I do feel loved and this is very comforting. Do you feel loved by God and Jesus?

Understanding this love, I am surrounded by comfort, care, and safety. There is the assurance that God and Jesus will not hurt me. Their only goal is to contribute to my comfort, joy, and happiness. They want me to feel good. This attracts me into their presence, a place where I delight to remain.

It is my intention to attract you there, to come into the presence of our Father, the home of love. It is also my intention in this book to walk us to the place where love grows sumptuously and shines brightly. In this place, human minds do not always agree on all levels, but because of the delightful distribution of LOVE, we cherish the presence and intentions of all who come here. So, come my friend, walk with me to the garden of love. Here, receive and give love.

You have not lived
Until for even a short moment,
You have lived in love.

Readers Notes –

"This book throbs with passion from a pastor's heart for the practice of love and graciousness in all congregational and personal relationships, especially when they get strained by misunderstandings and self-serving attitudes. This book contributes greatly to the discussion about personal conflict resolution from a pastoral and non technical point of view. It is personal, practical, spiritually motivated, and borne out of years of experience. One cannot read this book without wanting to be a better, kinder person, in all one's dealings with those about you."

Alf Birch, D. Min. Retired pastor and former Oregon Conference President.

"In these pages you find a pastor's heart revealed, that has been bathed and washed by the love of a Savior that he so obviously loves. Let his heart's concern take you into what it truly means for the church to be God's family."

Larry Gibson, pastor, Oregon Conference of Seventh-day Adventist.

"As Marriage and Family Educators, my wife and I are working to build living, lasting relationships. ***"Love Me With Tenderness"*** has great insight in dealing with family, church and the workplace. This book talks about difficult people and gives the readers the opportunity to learn about their personal attitude towards others as well as God's loving attitude toward them. The awareness this book creates will compel the readers to make life better for those around them. Thank you Ewart for showing us how to respond as Jesus did in changing lives that will contribute to growth, warmth, and friendship. When the church begins to live these principles of love, our churches will be over flowing. The results will be eternal and Jesus' Coming will be SOON!"

Harvey Corwin, Director of Family Ministries, Oregon Conference of Seventh-day Adventists.

"What a wonderful gift you have given everyone who reads your book. Those who take into their hearts and use the ideas and principles you have expressed will truly find the happiness, freedom and joy that God intends us to have here on this earth. With Christ as our guide, we can enjoy healthy, loving relationships while we prepare for the perfect relationships of heaven."

Julianne Fisher, East Salem Seventh-day Adventist Church member.

"Pastor Ewart Brown encourages us to love one another in spite of our differences and shows us how love, at work in our lives and our conversation, can transform our workplaces, our families, and our churches. His well-drawn scenarios show us why our natural responses to the things others say and do and believe may be counterproductive. With the insights we gain from reading this book, we are better able to reduce our frustration and the frustrations of others by finding tactful ways to approach people when we differ-and when we have already said and done things that have hurt another child of God. Pastor Brown's counsel gives the Spirit every opportunity to enter and heal our relationships. I recommend this book as a spiritual and practical guide to working well with others, whatever the relationship."

Nancy Cross, M.A., Director, Department of English, Walla Walla College.

Chapter 1

Love Someone Today. How?

Have you ever thought that a great definition for a Christian is, "Caring"?

Each new day is a day of challenges and opportunities. Some things will be just as a person desired. Other things will be less desired. Whatever is happening in an individual's life, you and I can make a positive impact upon that individual. And I am encouraging us to do just this. As we begin each new day, ask God to lead us to an individual or individuals whom we may love for Him, whose spirits we may encourage, whose burdens we may lighten and whose frowns we may change to smiles. People appreciate love.

People are longing for love. In this section, I have packaged for us little gems. Let us place these little gems in a corner of our memory bank and be ready to offer them to others as occasions come our way. I wish for us wisdom, tenderness, focus and fulfillment as we give away these love gems. Now here they are:

- Give away the very best we have to offer.
- Do good to at least one person each day.
- Give someone a portion of our happiness.

- Build someone's dream. Help someone to be successful.
- Give an appropriate hug.
- Be kind and tender.
- Be forgiving.
- Make someone feel special and valuable.
- Show that we genuinely care.
- Tune our ears to hear and our hearts to feel.
- Allow to fall from our lips only those words that tend to heal and encourage.
- Be like Jesus.
- Observe the good someone has done and take time to express our appreciation.
- Understand someone's point of view, even though we may disagree.
- Make time to listen to the heart that wants to talk.
- Write a short warm note and leave it on a desk or where it will be seen.
- Create an atmosphere for laughter.
- Speak nice things about someone.
- Love unconditionally.
- Offer an unexpected gift or compliment.
- If we have done wrong, apologize and ask for forgiveness.
- Keep a promise.
- Pray with someone.

As vegetation flourishes with care and water, so the human race lives a meaningful life when surrounded with loving words and behaviors. Again, I appeal to us to make a difference in someone's life by the way we love. And please let us remember, the love we give away will someday come back to us.

This past Christmas, Doug and Shirley, a couple at my church, gave me a gift and a card. The content of the card was especially warm. It was all compliments about me, thoughts that made me feel good inside. The thoughts were so good that I left the card sitting on my desk and read it several times. I decided that I will be keeping this card for a long time. It was too good to discard. What next did I do? I created a folder and named it "Happy File." I will keep in this Happy File, happy notes given to me. And when there are challenges in my life, I will go to my Happy File. Why not commit ourselves to contribute to someone's Happy File? The material we place into someone's file may someday walk back into ours.

The terrorists' attacks of September 11, 2001, have changed America and the world. We have been forced to see human existence in a different light. For in one moment there was life, and in another moment there was death. On that morning, if we had known that death was coming, we might have been nice to everyone we met and to those who walked into the World Trade Center, the Pentagon or boarded the planes. We would have spoken only nice, memorable words. We would have felt free to say:

"I love you."

"You have been a great person to me."

"I do appreciate you for all the wonderful things you do for me."

"I have never worked with someone as nice as you."

"My life has been changed because of you and I will forever be thankful."

"If I have done to you anything wrong, I am truly sorry. And will you please forgive me?"

We all are longing for love. We long for love today and each day. Let us not wait for the presence of disaster or death. Let us offer this love while it can be appreciated and enjoyed. Whom will you love today?

> Everyday, everywhere, someone is longing for love. Where will love come from if not from you and me?

There are individuals sharing our space at home, work, shopping mall, activity field or church needing us. Some of them are troubled, weary, and hurting, yet portray that all things are well and that they are happy, though deep down they are not. Only the sensitive eyes and tuned-in hearts are able to see beyond the colorful words and gestures and recognize what is really happening in these lives. They are calling for you and me to sense their pain and heal their brokenness. Therefore, I am calling upon us to -

Tame the moment

For those living in a wilderness,

For those within the windy clouds of emotion,

For those whose minds are anxious and restless,

For those whose minds are in fragments.

Let us

Defend and build their dreams,

Lift and sustain the falling hands of the burden bearer,

Paint smiles on the faces of the weather-beaten travelers,

Grease the emotional wheels of the squeaky pioneer,

Position ourselves in someone's presence until joy and smiles are born again,

Love someone for Jesus,

Mend a broken wing,

Build a haven of peace,

Be life savers and life givers.

And when someone steps away from our presence, having been touched by love, may the sentiments be expressed:

> "O how I have been loved. I actually felt loved. I grieve to see you go, but you have left with me a piece of you. And now, I am ready for my journey because of you."

> "I love you too, very much. The moment before you came was dark and cold, but you brought me warmth and light. My vision is now in focus. My courage is alive again. And with God and you close to me, it will be OK. Thanks much my friend."

There is a love story in the Bible that has touched my heart. Bible commentators have walked around it because it seemed so insignificant. And maybe it is. Yet when I read it, my heart cried. The story is about King Saul and his death. There was a servant who traveled with the king as he went to war. This servant was called the "Armor-Bearer." He carried weapons that protected the king when he faced danger. One day, in battle, the king was injured and would soon die. The king asked this servant to finish the death blow, so that the king would die instantly. But the servant would not, so the king killed himself. This servant must have been with the king for some time. My sense is that he was close to the king and maybe had loved the king. His heart could have been knit to the king. So was he broken when he looked and realized that the king was dead? Here is his touching response:

> ***"When his armor-bearer realized that Saul was dead, he fell on his own sword and died beside the king." 1 Samuel 31:5.***

Death might be more than what is expected of us. But this does show what love can do, even unto death. This is the nature of love which God has demonstrated for us:

> ***"For God so loved the world that he gave his only Son…." John 3:16.***
>
> ***"I command you to love each other in the same way that I love you. And here is how to measure it – the greatest love is shown when people lay down their lives for their friends." John 15:12, 13.***
>
> ***"We know what real love is because Christ gave up his life for us. And so we also ought to give up our lives for our Christian brothers and sisters." 1 John 3:16.***

Life is all about LOVE. In Thomas Kinkade's devotional book, *With Wings Like Eagles* he discussed the experience of love, mercy and justice in America. He said:

> *"…If God isn't pleased with America's sense of mercy and justice, there is no national dream of consequence."* (93)

On this statement I build my own:

> "If God is not pleased with the way Christians love each other, then there is no Christian service of consequence."

Loving someone is foundational to Christianity, the church and a successful, progressive society. Christianity and love are love-seat partners. Since love is so important, may our prayer be:

> "Lord, encase me with that mysterious aspiration to tame the turbulent winds of the soul.
> Shower me with that passion, until it becomes action.
> Place in my chest a heart like yours
> And take me to the streets to give it away."

Do you understand how it feels to be loved? If you do not, then do not give up. And I wish that experiencing love, is not too late for you. I wish that someone will love you, soon. If you have experienced love, then you know that the world is a beautiful place and there are music and flowers everywhere.

Yes, God has blessed me with people who do love me and show me love. Words are too few to describe the feeling of being loved. And let me say this, it does feel good to be loved, and I forever desire to be loved. And my heart tells me that I want to ***Love Someone***. Here is my prayer:

"Lord, lead me to someone whom I may love for you."

What is your desire or prayer? Everyday, everywhere, someone is longing for love. Where will love come from, if not from you and me?

Could the last days' conflicts be about how we love those whom Jesus has put beside us?

Reflection Page

- In your experience, do you know that you are loved and by whom?

- Have you ever observed how ones behavior changes when there is love? Explain.

- Is there someone whom you can love today or for whom you can do something special? Who may this person be and what will you do?

Chapter 2

Love Me with Tenderness

To love with tenderness is to help God spread Himself.

How do I desire to be loved? With tenderness. How do you desire to be loved? My guess is that you too desire to be ***Loved with Tenderness***. We all desire to be loved in such a way that leaves us feeling accepted and good. Several years ago, while living in Toronto, Canada, growing up in the Christian path was not easy. There were so many issues that I was dealing with that colored my perspective, and there was no one to really ease my pain nor give me any spiritual guidance. I found myself very involved in the youth activities of the church. I had tried to do what I thought was the best for the youth, but later discovered that my planned activities were considered inappropriate for the youth community. You may say, I got in trouble with the church. That's right. But no one had the courage to meet me and share any concerns with me. I simply heard along the way that there were concerns.

One sunny day, I was standing at the front of the church building under the bright heavens. It was a day I will always remember because of what Pastor Yauchtze said to me. Today, I wish I knew the location of Pastor Yauchtze so that he could hear the rest of the story.

At that meeting I told him that I was tired of being in trouble with the church. He knew all about the trouble that I was in and could have told me where I had gone wrong and how to think straight and do the right things. He did not tell me of my wrongs. He did not condemn me. He asked me one simple question, "Ewart, what is your relationship with Jesus?" There was no need to answer and I did not. I just thought on his question. I just loved him for being so kind to me. He ***Loved Me with Tenderness***. And I will always remember him for this. That moment with Pastor Yauchtze has always been with me, not only as a moment of ***Love with Tenderness***, but a moment which changed my relationship with Jesus to this very day. Jesus and Christianity became more meaningful to me since that moment. Thanks Pastor Yauchtze.

Take a moment to reflect on how Jesus loved the ones not deserving to be loved. Let us look to the last moment preceding His Calvary-cross journey. Jesus would have been heavily burdened with the weight of His mission, the sins of the world. We would think that He was focused with a single vision and emotionally charged. And usually when one is emotionally charged, there is the tendency to lose control. But will Jesus lose control of Himself and His emotions? Look for yourself.

The book of Matthew takes us to the scene. We call this scene, "The Last Supper." Here Jesus and His best buddies have come together for their final fellowship meal. There will never be another one like this. And there at the table was one dysfunctional friend, Judas. Jesus knew that, but no one else did. You and I would have avoided Judas and politely advised him to go home. We would not consider him deserving of this fellowship and would not want his influence to infect the other friends nor this sacred moment. But Jesus had no such thought about Judas. Let us observe how carefully and tenderly Jesus will deal with him.

> ***"When it was evening, Jesus sat down at the table with the twelve disciples. While they were eating, He said,***

> ***'The truth is, one of you will betray me.... One of you who is eating with me now will betray me.' " Matthew 26:20-23.***

If you were at the table with Jesus, if you were standing in the room observing, or if you were Judas sitting there, and heard that statement from Jesus, would you not be pleased with the way He handled the situation? I would be delighted and would have respected and loved Him even more. I suppose Judas died, knowing that he was ***Loved with Tenderness***. Notice, Jesus made His point to Judas but did not embarrass him. Thanks Jesus. And just think, Jesus would do the same for you and me. Isn't this nice? And would I do the same for you, or you for me?

Very shortly following this, Peter, a very close friend of Jesus, promised his forever faithfulness to Him. He was serious I do believe. But Jesus, knowing Peter, told him that his pledge of allegiance would fail that very night, before the rooster crowed (Matthew 26:33, 34). Jesus was right, for Peter disowned Him when He needed friends and support. But notice how Jesus dealt with Peter:

> ***"About an hour later someone else insisted, 'This must be one of Jesus' disciples because he is a Galilean, too.' But Peter said, 'Man, I don't know what you are talking about.' And as soon as he said these words, the rooster crowed. At that moment the Lord turned and looked at Peter. Then Peter remembered that the Lord had said, 'Before the rooster crows tomorrow morning, you will deny me three times.' And Peter left the courtyard, crying bitterly." Luke 22:59-62.***

Jesus could have said to Peter, "I told you so," or He could have expressed some language which would have caused Peter public embarrassment. But our Savior did not. Though I was not there to see Jesus' look, I can imagine His eyes were eyes of love, compassion and tenderness. And Peter must have been sorry for hurting the One who loved him so much.

Let us visit one more scene with Jesus. The book of John takes us to that scene. Here we find Jesus, early in the morning at the temple. He is sharing the good news with those who gathered. Here come some leaders of the church clutching within their grips a woman, whom they accused of sleeping with some man. These church leaders were pushing Jesus to give a death verdict for this woman, a verdict she did deserve. But as the crowd waited for the death verdict, they were astonished at the gentle response of Jesus. His response was as silent as writing. He began writing on the ground words that only the accused could appreciate. They, the accusers, very well understood what Jesus was writing, because the writing applied to them. Jesus did not need to utter a word to condemn them. They condemned themselves. And they went away ashamed, but relieved by the way Jesus handled the situation.

Now about the woman still standing among the crowd – yes, she had spent the night with a man and everyone knew this was wrong and deserving the death verdict. She expected Jesus to pronounce the death verdict upon her, but to her pleasant surprise, Jesus had something else in mind. Please listen:

> ***"…'Where are your accusers? Didn't even one of them condemn you?' 'No Lord,' she said. And Jesus said, 'Neither do I. Go and sin no more'." John 8:10, 11.***

Whether you are among the church leaders or you are the accused woman, I am sure you appreciate the manner in which Jesus handled the situation. He embarrassed no one. He called down no public judgment on any one, even though He could. What we see here is Jesus who loves people with tenderness. He deals with them with gentleness and compassion. In fact the Bible refers to Jesus as one who is compassionate. Did we not see a similar handling of an embarrassing situation in the beginning of time? There in the garden of Eden, Adam and Eve had broken trust with God by eating of the restricted fruit. Because of this, they hid themselves from God. Hear how God will handle these two embarrassed adults: ***"Where are you?" Gen. 3:9.*** Following this are a series of questions from God to them. There was no condemnation. You may read these questions in the later verses.

So now I ask, as Christians, followers of Jesus, how then are we to deal with the family of God? Or how do you desire to be treated? Has anyone ever dealt harshly with you and you cried or hurt and wished it was done differently? I have. And I am sure that you also have. It is for this reason that this book is written – that we all will become more intentional in loving the family of God with tenderness and gentleness.

How do I desire to be loved? ***With Tenderness***. Arriving at the church office one morning, I checked the messages on my answering machine. There were three special messages from three undisclosed individuals. The contents of the messages were that I was missed, that my involvement in the church life was appreciated and that my smiles were cheering. Oh, how encouraged I was after hearing this. I loved this. So would you. Let me here take time to say thanks to those three individuals who left such tender messages on my answering machine and also to the many others who have encouraged me along this troubled trail. At this very moment of writing, I just looked into my date book and there was a card someone sent to me. It was a note of appreciation and encouragement and I have kept it and read it from time to time. I tend to keep these kinds of notes. How about you?

When was the last time you told someone or wrote a note to someone to encourage or express your appreciation? It has been said that it is easier to criticize than to encourage. But may I suggest that it can be easier to encourage if one chooses to be an encourager. It is a joy to love and to encourage.

Never have I thought that I have been right in all my decisions. Like all of you, I have made mistakes. But these were not always detrimental. Mistakes are like ladders upon which one climbs to reach greater heights. It is said, "We learn from our mistakes." But how do we know when we have made them unless someone tells us? While I have sometimes been harshly criticized and condemned by my Christian family, what I would have appreciated was to be gently corrected with love and tenderness.

What I long for is this – that when I have done wrong, people will still love and understand me, and draw me into their hearts and invite me to take another look at my behavior. If I seem troubled, I want to be offered help. Then offer to walk with me, until I can see clearly.

What I long for is this – that when I have done wrong, people will tell me the truth, and please hand it to me in love. Speak nicely to me. I know from working with people that coarse, harsh and hurting words flow naturally and easily from our lips. Such words need neither planning nor preparation. Consider this: *Lester and Lenny had made arrangements to meet at the corner restaurant for lunch at 11:30 am. Lester arrived at 12:15 pm. He was late. Right? When Lester showed up, Lenny was already sitting in the restaurant and blurted out to Lester, without any efforts or thoughts, "Lester, you are always late. What's the matter with you?"

Notice how short and easy this statement is. On the other side, Lenny could have taken the time he had while waiting, and constructed another approach which could have been like this, "Lester, you had me worried when you did not show up at 11:30 as we had planned. Is everything all right?" Again, notice, this approach contained more words and took more time and effort. Also there was the possibility that Lenny's point to Lester might have been lost. But you know what? Building a good relationship is more important than making your point clear. And this is one of our grave problems, we tend to maximize clarity and truth, while we minimize relationships. We take the short way to get the work done at any cost, because we are so busy. Often it does not matter to us how our words affect another, so long as the point is made.

---

*You will read about Lester throughout this book. I have made him my favorite illustration. He will occasionally associate with Lenny and Lesmine.

What I long for is this – that when I have done wrong, someone will ***Love Me with Tenderness,*** that I will be spoken to nicely, that time will be taken to understand me. When someone has questions about my statements, to say to me, "Ewart, I am not at all understanding what you said. Will you give me some time to see if I can see it the way you do?" Yes, I will very much appreciate this response more than if it had been said, "I totally disagree with you. You are dead wrong. What you said made no sense to me at all." Think of this, which of these responses do we more often hear or experience? Which of the responses brings warmth to your heart? Which do you plan to adopt for your vocabulary as you deal with people? Paul reminded us of how Christian growth occurs. Listen please –

> ***"Instead, we will hold to the truth in love, becoming more and more in every way like Christ…." Ephesians 4:15.***

It is my intention to impress you with the tremendous truth about words. Words do have an impact on our hearers. Words will build or break. Why then do we not specialize in words and how they work? Recently, I encountered a story. Someone sent it to my wife via e-mail. In this story I will identify the two main characters as Lester and Lenny. Allow me to share this story with you.

Lester was a well respected, honest man with many characteristics a Christian should have, but he had never really connected to Christ, nor entered the door of the church. A few years earlier, after Lester and Lenny had spent time visiting, Lenny had asked him, "Lester, have you ever been to a church service in your life?" Lester hesitated. Then with a bitter smile, he told Lenny of his childhood experience some fifty years ago. He was one of many children in a large impoverished family. His parents had struggled to provide food, with little left for housing and clothing. When he was about ten, some neighbors invited him to worship with them. The Sunday School class had been very exciting! He had never heard such songs and stories before! He had never heard anyone read from the Bible!

After class was over, the teacher took him aside and said, "Son, please don't come again dressed as you are now. We want to look our best when we come into God's house." Lester stood in his ragged, unpatched overalls. Then looking at his dirty bare feet, he answered softly, "No ma'am, I won't ever." "And I never did," Lester said, abruptly ending the conversation.

Lester did show up at the church. The first time Lenny saw him at the church was on a Wednesday. Lester was in his mid 70's, with thinning silver hair and a neat brown suit. As Lenny looked at the immaculately dressed old gentleman lying in his casket, Lenny thought of the little boy of long ago. Lenny could almost hear Lester say, "No ma'am, I won't ever." And Lenny wept. This story challenges me, and hopefully you, to give attention to the words we speak, for words do have effect.

What I long for is this – that when I have done wrong, it does not become the talk of the town. No one helps me, the Lord, or themselves, when they choose to broadcast my wrong behaviors or poor choices to the community. For my opportunity to grow, might be affected by the community knowing about my wrong choices. What usually happens is this, the wider the range of gossip about me, the greater the number of individuals who will withdraw from me and distort my world. Can you see this happening to you or someone else?

Listen to what recently happened to me. I visited a church member who was a patient in the hospital. As we visited, my mind drifted away from his illness to some wrong choices this church member had made. No, I was not there when the church member had made those choices. Someone told someone and someone told me and who knows how many someones this information went through. Standing there by the hospital bed, I wished someone had not told me this piece of gossip. I did not need to know. Fortunately, I was able to reconnect with this sick person and minister to him.

What I long for is this – that when I have done wrong, someone will recognize my poor judgment, come to me with tenderness and help me to see the better way. As we reason together, just as the Lord and we reason together, I like to be drawn into a comfort zone, where I can trust the other person and know that my ultimate good is considered important. Please let me know that to err is the journey of humanity and that all of us do walk there. Comfort me. Do not chastise me. Chastisement embitters me and slows my growth. Let me know that on this human trail, if I should again fail, you will still be there for me. And if I should fail another time, you will still be there for me. Tell me that I need not fear whenever I see you coming, for you are the bearer of good news and tenderness. This is the path Jesus always walks for sinners.

What I long for is this – that when I have done wrong, someone will recognize my poor judgment and not only will come lovingly and tenderly to me, but will come as a friend. There is quite an impact when a rock hits against a rock compared with a butterfly landing on a rock. When a friend comes to meet a friend, the meeting tends to be soft and less threatening. So come as a friend. I will know that only good is meant for my life. Tell me with tenderness what I need to know and promise to stay with me as my friend. Promise to support me whatever my decisions may be, and if I have any questions or concerns, let me know that you will always be there for me. Also remind me of the other times when I made great and wise decisions so I will not forget I am capable of doing that. The visit which has the deepest touch is the one that affirms the good I have done. And when this is done you now have earned the license to visit with me again and help me work things through.

What I long for is this – that when I have done wrong, someone will recognize my poor judgment and come to me with tenderness in the name of a friend and will promise to be my prayer partner. Yes, I will need all the prayers to process the past and arrive at what is good and right. Prayers are our greatest tool. Prayers are the gateway to wisdom and to the heart of God. I will need to be assured that others are out there praying for me. Tell me once, tell me twice, tell me several times, write me notes, that you are praying for me and that everything will be alright.

This is how we love to be loved when we have done wrong– that people will come to us –

- Because they care about us, not because we have done wrong.
- Because they credit us with good intentions, not because we have broken the rules.
- Because they know there is a better way, not because they are set in their ways and only their ways are right.
- Because they desire for us to be bonded to Jesus and to each other, not because they want to change us.
- Because the Lord sent them to us, not because they are angry.

This section of the book is intended to attract all Christians to a godly, gentle and tender way to love others as we travel this journey where we all see things differently. My appeal is that we will forever reflect on the Biblical approach as is documented below:

> ***"We may know that these things make no difference, but we cannot just go ahead and do them to please ourselves. We must be considerate of the doubts and fears of those who think these things are wrong. We should please others. If we do what helps them, we will build them up in the Lord." Romans 15:1, 2.***
>
> ***"Dear brothers and sisters, if another Christian is overcome by some sin, you who are godly should gently and humbly help that person back into the right path…." Galatians 6:1.***
>
> ***"Most important of all, continue to show deep love for each other, for love covers a multitude of sins."***
> ***1 Peter 4:8.***

My appeal is that we will call upon God, asking Him to help us in our relationships with others. My heart's desire is that He will teach us how to love others with tenderness. My longing is that God will work with us to create an environment so that when a person leaves our presence, that person will feel good, that person will see life as a jewel or pearl to be enjoyed or sought after, because there was love, tender love.

How do you desire to be loved?
How will you give love?
Can you think of a special person
who desires to be
Loved with Tenderness?

If no one loves you with tenderness,
then it is your turn to love with tenderness.
The world may not change, but you can.

Reflection Page

- Do you experience God to be tender and gentle? Please describe.

- Can you recall the times in your life when you were treated tenderly and warmly? When?

  a.____

  b.____

  c.____

  d.____

- If possible, discuss with someone the way Jesus dealt with Judas and Peter. Express what you really liked about His method.

- What additional thoughts do you have about the subject of this chapter?

Chapter 3

The Little Things

Who will have a brighter tomorrow, because I spent my today with them?

It has been said that it is easier to hurt than to heal. This means that it is natural to hurt someone, it takes no effort. But it takes an intentional effort to bring happiness to someone. Many have found this to be true. Have you? This section of this book is intended to invite us to be intentional in saying and doing good things for others, for the good we do or say will brighten the day for someone. Why not try to do even a little thing for the people who come into your space?

Several individuals have done ***Little Things*** for me, and I will forever remember them. And even more than ***The Little Things*** they did, I am touched by the love that motivated their behavior. I am including just a few of ***The Little Things*** that people have done for me, hoping that you will be inspired to do similar things for others.

☆ While pastoring the Lents church in Portland, Oregon, my family and I had taken a vacation trip to Jamaica, my birth place. After two weeks away, we had arrived at the Portland airport at midnight, having traveled since early that morning. We hurried from the plane, tired but glad to be home. Arriving at the waiting area, we were welcomed with the words and joyous tones, “Welcome Home.” Yes, very much alive and enthusiastic, were members of the Lents church family, with a banner held high with welcome home language. How sweet that was of these friends. I will forever remember this event and the faces there that night. Thanks friends.

☆ It was a Sunday morning and it was my birthday. The deaconesses were having a meeting, and I was invited to attend. So I showed up. On the head table was an interesting sight. Someone thought that I would sit there or that the object sitting there would surely be seen by me. You would never guess what was there for me. It was a huge eggplant with two candles. You see, my friend Billie knew that eggplant is surely not my delight. In fact, I will never eat this object. But please know that later she added to the table a delicious serving of my favorite, carrot cake. Such humor is unforgettable. I am so thankful for these fine friends.

☆ Talking about eggplant, there was another eggplant occasion. I was a relief chaplain at the Adventist hospital in Portland, Oregon. One Tuesday morning I went to chaplain’s meeting. There sitting on the table, where it was believed that I would sit, was a huge eggplant with a bow taped on the top. This was done for me. Beulah knew that eggplant was not my delight. This brought so much laughter and relaxation. Several months later, I preached a sermon and was able to use this eggplant story. The sermon was titled, “Eggplant with a bow on top.” Occasionally someone meets me and reminds me of the eggplant sermon. Thanks Beulah

☆ We met for Bible study that Sabbath morning. I mentioned that in Jamaica, my favorite drink was a non alcoholic ginger drink. But I have not found it here in North America. Just a few days later, there was a box at my door – 12 bottles of ginger drinks. Thanks Dan and Lavella.

☆ Linda must have also heard that I enjoy ginger drink. So one Sabbath morning she stopped by my office with a gift for me. It was a bottle of ginger drink. Thanks Linda.

☆ The tie-tack belonged to her husband who had died. Most people would choose to keep this forever. But rather than keeping it for ever, she chose to share it with me.
Thanks Winifred.

☆ My dear wife, Lynn, knows that carrot cake is my favorite. While at work she went to the cafeteria for supper. She remembered to bring me, wrapped in love, a slice of carrot cake. Thanks Lynn, my Love.

☆ One evening while at the church, Debbie said she had something for me. She had gone to Portland that day. Remembering my delight, she brought for me a delicious slice of carrot cake, with even a fork. Thanks Debbie.

☆ This day, the telephone call was different. For Freda said she had nothing in particular to talk about. She just wanted to say hello to me. "Hello Freda." And thanks.

☆ I attended a concert one Saturday evening held in the school gymnasium. Most of the seats were taken, so I remained standing at the back, undecided about where to sit. It was announced that seats were scarce and those with available seats beside them to make it known. Gary raised his hand and waved it several times at me, inviting me to sit with him. I felt good. Thanks Gary.

☆ Church service concluded and majority of the worshippers had left. I had planned to remain at the church since in a short time I would need to be there for a memorial service. Doug knew of my plan and had a different idea. He invited me to his home that was closer to the church. There I enjoyed a warm meal and fellowship. Thanks Doug.

☆ This has never happened before. Now it happens every Sabbath morning, with a few exceptions. At about 7:30 a.m., Leroy calls, just to pray with Lynn and me as we face the Sabbath day. This is very special. We do thank you, Leroy.

☆ On the day of my birthday, I chose to be in the church office. That Wednesday, Janet informed me that I needed to be in the office at noon. Standing at the door were four precious smiling little faces of girls with their mom, grandfather and goodies for my birthday, singing "Happy Birthday." Thanks Barb and family.

☆ I went to the drive up station at Taco Bell and ordered my lunch. As I drove to the window to receive my order the car in front of me caught my attention. The face in the driver's side mirror looked familiar. When I got to the window to pay, the attendant told me that the lady in the car ahead, who had already driven away, had paid for my lunch. Though I was in a car she had never seen me drive before she still recognized me. Thanks Brenda.

☆ Before Lynn and I left for California, where I would do a concert, I had requested that those in the church office pray for me. I wanted this concert to be an opportunity for ministry, therefore prayer was very essential. Further more I had just been afflicted with a sore throat, and you know what this means to singing. Upon returning to the church office, even before the traditional greetings after being gone, the first question asked of me was, "How was the concert?" The people in the office cared about that which was important to me. I particularly expressed to them my thanks for their interest. Thanks Gary and Janet.

☆ I have received only one real trophy in my lifetime. It happened at the cricket banquet where I was awarded for being the bowler of the year. How did this happen? As a little boy, I grew up playing the game of cricket. A few years ago, I was invited to visit a cricket game. This was my delight, since I had not played for many years. Arriving on the cricket field, Cam met me and invited me to join them in the game. I did. Shortly after positioning myself, Shaun asked me if I bowled. I informed him that I had bowled in the past, many years ago. So he invited me to bowl. I resisted. He invited me again and again and again. And I could no longer resist. So I agreed to bowl. The truth is, I really wanted to bowl but I was a coward, since I was a stranger on the field. So I bowled and did well. They marveled at my performance. So did I. They counted on me to bowl for the team. They recognized me as one of their star bowlers. And I was able to produce. That's why I was chosen as the bowler of the year. What if Shaun had not encouraged me to bowl? Shaun, I do thank you for believing in me and encouraging me.

☆ The gift of a rose – Lynn told me of this: She was walking to her exercise center one morning when she met a gentleman who was in his electric wheel chair and using nasal oxygen. He had in a little basket suspended on the front of his wheel chair several roses from his garden. He took a rose out of his basket and handed it to Lynn. Well, this was his way of bringing brightness and love to someone's life. I suppose several individuals received roses that day. Lynn was so impressed about the little deed of love that she took time to tell me about it. Thanks sir.

☆ Steven is a friend of mine. One morning I called him and sang "Happy Birthday." He was very surprised since I had not spoken with him for several months. He expressed how much he appreciated my thinking of him on his birthday. What touched me was when he said that he was very discouraged about life that morning and he did not desire to continue living. Earlier that day he had told one of his relatives that this was going to be his last birthday. But because of my call and song, he now felt life was worth living and he was willing to continue. He repeatedly thanked me for the call and song. From this experience I learned that a simple telephone call remembering something special does make a difference. It could save someone's life.

☆ I had worked in the Spokane area as a pastor for three years. The people there were good to me. But the time had come for my family and me to relocate in Oregon. Twelve years after we had left Spokane, I met with a group of pastors from the Northwest. This meeting was warm since past friendships were rekindled. But what touched me most was this statement made to me, "Ewart, you are still missed in Upper Columbia." It took just a few seconds to say this to me, but it left me with a mountain of good feelings. Thanks, Max, for taking time to say this.

This is just a very small sample
of ***The Little Things*** people do.
Thanks for all the many other unmentioned
expressions of love from many of you.

I will remember the things you said.
I will remember the things you did.
But I will especially remember
how you made me feel.
Thanks, with love.

Reflection Page

- Can you recall several little things others did for you that brought you joy? Name just a few if you can:

  a.____________________________________

  ____

  b.____________________________________

  ____

  c.____________________________________

  ____

- Do you remember brightening someone's day by doing little deeds of kindness? Namely-

  a.____________________________________

  ____

  b.____________________________________

  ____

  c.____________________________________

  ____

- Today, can you give away a little love? And if you do what will it do to your heart?

Chapter 4

A Story about Friends

Friendship is blind to hardship and walks with you through the valley of pain.

A friend sent me an e-mail. She indicated that the message was touching and even pushed a few tears from her eyes. After reading her e-mail, I understood why my friend was touched, for I too was touched, and I now want to share it with you. See where you are in this story. The story is titled, "That's What Friends Do" and here it is, as it appeared:

"Jack tossed the papers on my desk – his eyebrows knit into a straight line as he glared at me. 'What's wrong?' I asked. He jabbed a finger at the proposal. 'Next time you want to change anything, ask me first,' he said, turning on his heels and leaving me stewing in anger.

"How dare he treat me like that, I thought. I had changed one long sentence, and corrected grammar – something I thought I was paid to do. It's not that I hadn't been warned. The other women, who had served in my place before me, called him names I couldn't repeat. One co-worker took me aside the first day. 'He's personally responsible for two different secretaries leaving the firm,' she whispered.

As the weeks went by, I grew to despise Jack. It was against everything I believed in – turn the other cheek and love your enemies. But Jack quickly slapped a verbal insult on any cheek turned his way. I prayed about it, but to be honest, I wanted to put him in his place, not love him.

"One day, another of his episodes left me in tears. I stormed into his office, prepared to lose my job if needed, but not before I let the man know how I felt. I opened the door, and Jack glanced up. 'What?' he said abruptly. Suddenly I knew what I had to do. After all, he deserved it. I sat across from him. 'Jack, the way you've been treating me is wrong. I've never had anyone speak to me that way. As a professional, it's wrong, and it's wrong for me to allow it to continue,' I said. Jack snickered nervously and leaned back in his chair. I closed my eyes briefly. God help me, I prayed. 'I want to make you a promise. I will be a friend,' I said. 'I will treat you as you deserve to be treated, with respect and kindness. You deserve that,' I said. 'Everybody does.' I slipped out of the chair and closed the door behind me.

"Jack avoided me the rest of the week. Proposals, specs, and letters appeared on my desk while I was at lunch, and the corrected versions were not seen again. I brought cookies to the office one day and left a batch on Jack's desk. Another day I left a note. 'Hope your day is going great,' it read. Over the next few weeks, Jack reappeared. He was reserved, but there were no other episodes. Co-workers cornered me in the break room. 'Guess you got to Jack,' they said. 'You must have told him off good.' I shook my head. 'Jack and I are becoming friends,' I said in faith. I refused to talk about him. Every time I saw Jack in the hall, I smiled at him. After all, that's what friends do.

"One year after our 'talk,' I discovered I had breast cancer. I was 32, the mother of three beautiful young children, and scared. The cancer had metastasized to my lymph nodes and the statistics were not great for long-term survival. After surgery, I visited with friends and loved ones who tried to find the right words to say. No one knew what to say. Many said the wrong things. Others wept, and I tried to encourage them. I clung to hope.

"The last day of my hospital stay, the door darkened and Jack stood awkwardly on the threshold. I waved him in with a smile and he walked over to my bed and, without a word, placed a bundle beside me. Inside lay several bulbs. 'Tulips,' he said. I smiled, not understanding. He cleared his throat. 'If you plant them when you get home, they'll come up next spring.' He shuffled his feet. 'I just wanted you to know that I think you'll be there to see them when they come up.' Tears clouded my eyes and I reached out my hand. 'Thank you,' I whispered. Jack grasped my hand and gruffly replied, 'You're welcome. You can't see it now, but next spring you'll see the colors I picked out for you.' He turned and left without a word. I have seen those red and white striped tulips push through the soil every spring for over ten years now. In fact, this September the doctor will declare me cured. I've seen my children graduate from high school and enter college.

"In a moment when I prayed for just the right word, a man with very few words said all the right things. After all, that's what friends do."

This story paints the picture of what this book is all about. You and I do live and relate to individuals who present us with challenges. Our book of deeds is well supplied with how to respond to these challenging individuals. And often it is just a matter of turning the page to find a response. But not all responses are the right, gracious, tender and God-like ones.

My loving, touching request is that we will love with tenderness, that we will respond to challenging individuals in ways that will contribute to growth, warmth and friendship, just as Jesus would and just as we would like for ourselves. And when the exchange is all over, Jesus will say, "Friend you have done just as I would. I am proud of you."

I personally have accepted this challenge. Will you join me?

Reflection Page

❖ Do you have a friend who is patient with you?

❖ Sometimes the way we react to a situation is colored by what we have been told previously. Is this true for you? When did you experience this?

❖ What story can be told about your friendship, or any friendship?

Chapter 5

Working with a Difficult Person

Love plants flowers even in a landfill.

Have you ever had the privilege of ***Working with a Difficult Person***? If your answer is "yes," no doubt you are beginning to recall the face, challenge, pain and growth. I have never met anyone who delights in ***Working with a Difficult Person***. My memory tells me that difficult people are usually left behind. We just don't bother with them, or we simply tolerate them, hoping that they will vanish. I, too, have poorly dealt with the difficult person and have unfairly related to him. This was not right. And if you are presently ***Working with a Difficult Person*** and have read the works of other authors on the subject, simply consider my contribution as an addition. This comes from my own experience, and I want to tell you that what you are about to read does work for me. Something here might work for you.

As I think of a difficult person, in no way am I suggesting that this person is bad or in any way a step down from another. Not at all. By my definition, the difficult person is the one with whom you and I associate but feel tension in the relationship. The person just does not seem to understand you, is not easily pleased, is often angry and disagreeable and is always complaining. You may have other descriptions as well.

As you work with this difficult person (perhaps Lester), you might need to apply all of the following thoughts, or just the ones you consider appropriate. Here they are:

Face Lester and the issue - Seize the opportunity to *carefront him. Tell him that you are bothered by his behavior. Be specific about the behavior and your feelings, but in all this, be loving and tender.

Love Lester – You do not have to be a best friend to him, but as Jesus would, love him. Be a friend. Be courteous and kind. Create those occasions that will tend to build friendship between you and him.

Forgive Lester - He might not realize the effects of his behavior. He might be innocent. So treat him as though he were not responsible for his behavior. And if he were not responsible, then why not forgive him? And even if he were responsible, forgive him as well. Then treat him as though his intentions were meant only for your good.

Understand Lester - Reason that he has had good days but that today was just a bad day and when things are bad, everything goes wrong. Tomorrow will be a better day for him. Then he will be more reasonable and flexible.

Pray for Lester - Talk to God about him as you would talk about a friend. The power of God enables us to relate better to the ones we are praying for. It is difficult to pray for a person you don't like.

Engage Lester – Do not ignore him. Intentionally invite him to your home or to an event where you will be

---

*Carefront – A loving form of confronting, further explained in the chapter "I Have Been Hurt-What Do I Do?"

present. When you walk by him, take a quick moment to connect with him. Even a touch on the shoulder will do.

Praise Lester – Take time to praise him for the good things he has done or is doing. Love tends to follow and responds to praise. He might be a difficult person simply because he does not like you or because you do not like him. But if you praise his work, he is more likely to like you.

Surprise Lester – Know what he likes. Do something nice to surprise him. This may be a gift, a card or even a telephone call. Show him that you care about him. Love is the torch that melts iron when nothing else can.

Speak positively of Lester – If the subject of Lester comes up in conversation with others, speak only positively of him.

Recognize Lester's strengths – There are things which he does very well and loves to do. Identify these strengths and let him know that you are aware of them. Praise him for these and allow him to use them if possible. Solicit his opinions, for he has insights. Tell others about the things he does well.

Be patient with Lester – He may strike when you are at your low point of the day. And you might be unprepared for his behavior, or you might be enjoying the splendor of the moment. At any of these moments you might be tempted to respond to him in a harsh way. This will not work. Instead, be patient with him. Give him time. But be firm and pleasant. Never give up on him. Stay with him as together you process away the pain.

Be straight with Lester – If he works for you, tell him exactly what you want done. Make sure there is no misunderstanding in your expectation or interaction. Clear direction is easier to follow, to explain and to defend. But in doing this, it is important to maintain his integrity. Do not treat him as a child.

Be true to yourself – It is not necessary to lower your standards or change your expectations simply to appease Lester. If that is done, he has no incentive to grow, and he will take pride in his victories over you. Know who you are. Recognize your true feelings. Be confident about your work. As you state your positions and expectations, do so clearly and with tenderness, then expect the appropriate response. Do not be wishy-washy.

Trust God with Lester – There are times when all our efforts will result in failure. Nothing seems to work. He is just as difficult as ever. Well, this is not the time to retire to hopelessness and despair. No, this is the time to say, "God, I am placing Lester in your hands." Then please remember to leave him there.

After you have tried everything and nothing seems to have worked with Lester, this difficult person, may I suggest that you try two things:

1. Pray for strength, wisdom and patience to work with him in a loving way.
2. Look at yourself, to see if the difficult person might be you. Could it be?

Working with a Difficult Person – Where do we expect to find this person? We will find the difficult person anywhere there are people. He is unavoidable. And may I suggest, he does not have to be a pain, but instead he can be an opportunity. We can use this challenge of ***Working with a Difficult Person***, as an opportunity to teach that person how to treat us. We can also use this challenge to see what is inside of us. As we work with the difficult person, there will be moments of discouragement and frustration, but please, let us not be overcome by these. Instead, let us make a conscious choice of how we will react to him. Build the wall before the rush of water. I think of the times when I will be facing the difficult person. I tell myself that there is no reason to face the moment with a frown. Therefore, I prepare and polish my mannerism, smiles and words to meet the moment. And when the moment comes, I am able to conduct myself with ease and smiles. Why? I am ready for the moment. Well, you may rightly ask, "How many times can one do this?" You are right, not many. But hopefully, there will not be the need for many.

Another thought – Is it possible that my prejudices towards Lester are obvious to him and that he is consciously or subconsciously reacting to who I am? Is it possible that I might be the one contributing to his behavior? But what if the problem is Lester? Then let us see this whole challenge of him as an adventure, one to be pursued until the gold is found.

It is true that ***Working with a Difficult Person*** is a challenge or a pain for some. But it is also true that people are not always what they appear to be. Deep down they are gold, just craving for love, friendship and recognition. Therefore, let God lead us to the gold. Let God cast before us the picture of what one can become and not what one is. It is human to see what one is, but it is divine to see what one can become. Let God cast before us the joys that come from a battle won, so that we will be encouraged to continue fighting and to realize that the battle is worth it. Remember, the joy is not in the battle, but in the battle won. As we fight this battle or face this challenge of ***Working with a Difficult Person***, may we wear as our armor the loving Jesus Christ, our Lord and Savior.

Working with a Difficult Person
Who is that difficult person?
Well, I sometimes wonder,
What does God think of me?

> As we travel through the meadow of caring for others, it is then that we behold the glory and beauty of God.

Reflection Page

- ❖ Can you identify a difficult person with whom you have worked or with whom you are presently working?

- ❖ Why was the individual difficult to work with?

- ❖ What information in this chapter might be most helpful to you as you work with the difficult person?

- ❖ Are there any benefits from working with a difficult person?

- ❖ What changes can I make as I work with the difficult person?

Chapter 6

Safe, Sweet Home

Home is –
A safety blanket
A security blanket
A teddy bear.

There is something special about home. When things are going wrong at the work place or school, there often comes an urge to go home. Why home? Home is that place that represents trust and safety. Home is that place where everything will be all right. I do have clear memories of my boyhood days when I got in trouble with one of my peers but was not able to handle him because he was stronger than me. So I invited him to follow me. And I remained innocent and helpless until I reached my home. Upon reaching home, I was transformed. I was ready for war and victory. I knew that I could handle anything while I was home. Now that I am grown I fight different kinds of battles. And home continues to be that place that I desire, where I will find peace, trust and rest. I do hope that you have this kind of home to come to after a complex, crucifying day.

This section, however, will not attract you to our homes, the places of residence, though it might apply. Instead, I hope to attract you to the Christian's second home, the church. We will look at the church as a ***Safe, Sweet Home***. This is the place we come to each week. Some come here several times each week, not only to worship and find God, but to find rest and peace. You see, the experiences of life are very trying. We daily deal with issues relating to finance, family, work place, health, people and more. And many of us are weary from trying to cope. So we come to the church for strength, rest and encouragement, hoping to grasp enough that will propel us to face another day or week. We know that the church will offer what no other place on earth can offer, and that is why we come week after week and year after year.

Let me ask, do you remember the times when you came to church and found it as safe and sweet as your home? Or do you remember the times when you came to church and found it a cold, lonely and frightening place to be, because you trusted no one and no one trusted you? Do you remember the times when you came to church with a broken heart, hoping for healing from a human being, but no one connected with you? And how did you feel? It is my sense that God always connects with the heart that reaches out to Him. But when other human beings fail to connect with us, a shadow seems to come between us and God. When we touch each other and love each other, we have a deeper appreciation for God. We see God more clearly.

> If God wanted an ambassador
> through whom to send His love to mankind,
> would He choose you or me?

For the past forty-five years, I have been a part of this great family, called the church. You and I have heard others describe the church family as "a place of worship," "a place where God meets the people," "a hospital for the sick," "a hospital for sinners," and so forth. All these descriptions are appropriate. But how many people are able to say that the church is for them a place of safety and sweetness? In this section, we will focus on the church or the church family as a place that is ***Safe and Sweet***.

The subject of safety is a friend of our culture. Let me cite just a few safety engines in our society: The industrial market, automotive market, neighborhood and communities, airplane industry, home builders industry, insurance companies, and even churches. These and more have a primary interest in safety, for safety saves lives and money. Our Government spends millions of dollars to give the American public a sense of safety. The presence of a law enforcement officer gives us a sense of safety. Sky marshals in airplanes give us a feel of safety.

My church headquarters in the state of Oregon has strongly suggested that each local church organize a Safety Committee. This committee is to see that safety is practiced in the church, for safety saves lives and money. My local church has a Safety Committee. We do our best to remove hazards. We put in place mechanisms that will insure safety, for we want individuals to feel safe when we gather for worship or fellowship. And yet there is another safety factor to which we often give little attention. Let me introduce this factor by asking, Do you feel safe from emotional hazards when you come to church? Do you feel free to be yourself in the presence of diversity? I wish I could hear your answer.

Would you agree that the emotional safety of the worshipper deserves primary attention? Would you agree that people's hearts and how they feel when they come to worship deserve primary attention? Would you agree that worship is difficult when an individual feels accepted by God but not by the worshippers around her? Would you also agree that, in fact, a worshipper who feels unsafe may even refuse to come to church? If your answers are as I assumed they would be, then it is time to give primary attention to the subject of making worship and the church family ***Safe and Sweet***.

Please allow me to expose my heart in an attempt to respond to the above concern. As a pastor working with people, I have learned that many see the church as a very unsafe place.

I regret saying this. Those who find the church to be unsafe are the ones who sometimes leave, maybe wandering from church to church, or who may remain in the church with deep pain.

Many leave the church not because of doctrinal discrepancies, but because they have been hurt by church members. Does this sound familiar? It is so true that many of us love our church and have done much for her. We desire to forever joyfully dedicate our time and means towards her growth. But when we are hurt by members, our spirits are hijacked, our passions are deflated, and it takes more than human powers to keep us coming back.

If you are one of those who have been hurt by a church member, you know exactly what I am saying. I have often heard it said, "My church is not kind." or "My church has been hard on me." My plea to the Christian community is this, that all of us become intensely aware of human emotions and needs, and that we become intentional about caring for our church family. It is very possible that the last days' conflicts may have something to do with how we care about others. Therefore, let us cut back on hurting people and step up on nurturing and up-building.

It hurts me to think of this and even worse to write it, but here it is: If Lester had known of how he would have been treated within the church family, he may never have joined. For he thought that the church family was not only a God-like place, but a ***Safe and Sweet Home***. He was told that in the church he would find things different from in the "world." People would be kind, patient and compassionate. But shortly after Lester was planted in the family, he found himself the object of rash criticism, cruel judgment and shunning.

Would you believe that so many of us who consider ourselves to be Christians, who teach the Bible and morality, are the same ones whose behavior and language pierce the hearts of other mortal flesh? How could this happen? How could a good Christian be so careless in dealing with another Christian? And why do some church members say that the worst treatment they ever received came from their church family? I cannot understand. Do You?

> Lord, teach me to love You.
> Lord, teach me to love others.
> Lord, stretch my borders
> and fill me with tenderness.
> Lord, send me like the scented wind
> to shape lives with tenderness,
> love, and compassion.

For several minutes, I have attempted to engage you in the subject of safety and sweetness of our church family. It is appropriate to ask the question, "What does Ewart mean by ***Safe and Sweet***?" Well, let me, in a brief moment share with you from my heart what I mean. When I think and write about a church that is ***Safe and Sweet***, I am describing a church where certain ingredients are present and experienced. I call these, "Ten Roses in a Church Garden." As we apply these to our church families, we will find that our church will be transformed into a ***Safe and Sweet Home***. Some of you are already experiencing this. God bless your family and growth. For you who are open to traveling on this exciting, growing and enriching experience, here are the "Ten Roses in a Church Garden." This list is only a beginning:

1. Fellowship Love – Many of us within our church family are saturated with Bible truths. We have enough Bible information. But what we dearly desire is to feel that we belong and that we are important. When we walk into the church building, we want someone to become excited because we are there. We desire to be invited for fellowship, for a meal, on a shopping spree, or maybe just for a drive in the country. Added to that, we will welcome a surprise telephone call during the week just to say, "Hi, I care and I am wondering how you are doing today." We desire to have friends who will do things with us. Many church members who sit beside us in the pews are lonely. Lonely people talk and smile as if everything is fine, but often they are not. Loneliness brings pain, and the lonely are calling for fellowship and inclusion. Fellowship Love packages loneliness and piles it beyond a concrete barricade, and scarcely will loneliness again surface its ugly head. Therefore let us give away Fellowship Love in great abundance.

2. Giving Love – People who are in love may enjoy shopping for each other. We know of the magic of a gift. A gift says that love is real and goes to a greater extent. A gift says, you mean so much to me, I want you to remember that I care. When words might be forgotten gifts will be remembered. And remember, the receiver is not looking for a price tag just a heart extended. The love that goes furthest maybe the love accompanied with a gift. Have you personally experienced this to be true?

3. Listening Love – It does really matter that we are listening. We are listening because we care. No, we might not have answers, but we have the time to listen. It is peaceful to know that someone loves us so much as to listen to us. Someone loves us so much as to stop whatever activity is occurring, just to listen to us. We call this undivided attention. Listening Love concentrates upon hearing the words of the heart. Listening Love hears beyond what the lips say. It demonstrates interest and asks questions to facilitate comfortable conversations. And the good news is that this love does not condemn, it loves and listens and seeks to understand. One who is being listened to will come back for another round of talks. For in listening, we give not only our ears, but our hearts. It is quite a compliment to hear one say, "I love her because she listens to me."

4. Nurturing Love – While there is life there is growth. And why does the fruit tree grow? Because someone provided watering, pruning and caring. We as human beings were created to grow. We grow when we are challenged, encouraged, supported and loved. We cherish the questions that entice us to think things through and arrive at conclusions because of the process. We welcome encouragement. So let us speak of the good accomplished and greater goals will be set and pursued. It pays to focus on building others. For building others builds a church, a home, a community and a country. The ones we build may one day return to build us.

5. Kindness Love – Every heart cries out for and appreciates kindness. This world and culture often prey on us with vengeance, and we are crushed. Therefore we stretch out our hands and hearts for kindness. We desire that whatever is done is done with tenderness and kindness. I am hoping and praying that the words we speak, the deeds we perform, the sentiments we spread all flow like rivers of kindness. The apostle Paul knew of the power of kindness, thus he wrote:

> ***"Instead, be kind to each other, tender hearted, forgiving one another…." Ephesians 4:32.***

Where there is kindness, there is Christ. Where there is kindness, there is life. Seemingly, everything grows well where kindness is long and indifference is short. Should we then not cultivate kindness? Should we then not seek to still the wars of the mind with kindness and gentleness? Should we then not seek to sweeten the toils of daily life with down-pours of kindness? Let us cherish the behavior of Jesus. He was kind. Even when He found it necessary to rebuke someone, He did it with kindness.

Be kind, it is the Christian thing to do,
for we desire the happiness of others.
Be kind, it is the social thing to do,
for we respect the thoughts and actions of others.
Be kind, it is the right thing to do,
for God is kind.
The world and its arteries lack kindness,
but let the church be the mother of kindness.

> Lord, in all my dealings with those You send to me, please let me perfume them with loving kindness.

This should be a noble commentary about every one of us: "Above everything that he does, he is always a kind person."

6. Acceptance Love – In the book, *Love, Acceptance & Forgiveness,* by Jerry Cook and Stanley C. Baldwin is this line: *"When we cultivate the habit of accepting people, they open up to us, they like us, they trust us instinctively."* (7) Have you found this to be true? When we embrace the thought of acceptance, we recognize that among us are individuals who are different, difficult, abandoned or sinners.

These are on another level from where we stand and sometimes these individuals feel that they are outsiders, that they do not belong. Acceptance to these individuals means knowing they are welcomed and that they are all right, they are a special gift from God just as they are, they are loved regardless, they are at the right place with the right people. Acceptance Love knows no differences. Acceptance Love knows only oneness and equality.

7. Forgiveness Love – Forgiveness Love invites us to be ourselves and not attempt to be God. We will not cast judgment on others. We will not encase our brother or sister in a box colored with our own personal prejudices. Rather we will release him or her who has wronged us. We will treat the offender as though we are friends, as though there was never a bitter moment between us. Forgiveness is like the dew of the morning, the smiles of the rising sun, the music in the flower garden, a child playing in the sand on the beach. Forgiveness is a baby being born. Forgiveness is love. In the church family where there is forgiveness, there is God, and we know that we are loved. In the church family where there is forgiveness, the Lord will send people who are hurting and who need a God-like touch. Forgiveness can be a gathering tool, an evangelistic tool.

8. Honesty Love – Honesty Love is a rare commodity because we fear we will offend when we tell the truth. We know that something needs to be said, but how will it be said or who should make the contact? Because we have not mastered the art of carefronting, we sometimes choose the path of "ignoring."

Honesty Love is an appeal to us to cultivate the heart to express our concerns with kindness and love rather than to ignore and remain silent. For we grow out of our weaknesses when we are informed, especially if the information comes packaged in love and kindness.

There are times when it pays to be silent, especially when speaking will make the mud become muddier. However, many individuals would welcome hearing the true content of our hearts. Let us with the lips and heart of Jesus connect with those the Lord has sent to us and help them grow. Let us love them. They will love us because we helped them to see who they really are and where they can be with God's help and our support. So please tell the truth, in love.

9. Carefronting Love – David Augsburger said: *"Carefronting is the way to communicate with both impact and respect, with truth and love. 'Speaking the truth in love' is the way to mature right relationships."* Wherever there is a community, there is conflict. As Christians, we are vulnerable to disagreements and conflicts. We do see things differently. The question is: When we are in the maze of disagreements, how do we get out? Carefronting Love is one good way. For Carefronting Love escorts us to come face to face with the person or persons involved and lovingly process the problem. We neither run away nor hide from the problem. Neither do we short circuit the process, but we lovingly and patiently work the process until all parties are friends again. Carefronting Love is as a medicine, like healing oil on a wound. Many avoid this process, but it is essential to community growth and health.

10. Touching Love – Touching Love is Christian Love. This is a love that is discreet, deep, perceptive and patient. This is a love born in the heart of God and transmitted to humanity. And when this love is placed in our bosom, we feel warm, cuddled, elevated and special. We are dressed with smiles, laughter and purpose. We see beauty emanating from the rough, rugged and ragged. We see God and feel His presence. We see the world differently and see God's people as our friends. We see the world, a vibrant, verdant habitat as God's creation, just because love has fallen upon us. This love cannot be pictured by words or art. No, it unfolds itself only in an experience. One only feels this love and knows that this is what is needed and more is desired. Those of us who have been recipients of this love know that it sometimes pushes tears from our eyes. We are so loved and we are so happy and we are so touched. When words cannot vent our thoughts, the trickling tears do. This is Touching Love.

O love, sweet love, ever fall on me.
O love, sweet love, flow from me to you.

I hope you found the "Ten Roses in a Church Garden" beneficial. Which roses did you recognize as being present in your church family? And which do you need to plant? Hopefully you found these challenging enough to make a difference in your community.

Having stepped out of the Rose Garden, allow me to take you to another called the "Trust Garden". We are now entering the "Trust Garden". This is where we find the bottom line of relationships and what constitutes Safety and Sweetness within the church family. The church family is built upon Christ and trusting relationships. From Webster's dictionary, I have gleaned that trust has to do with: reliability, integrity, surety, guardianship and dependence as they relate to human communities. This means that within our church family, we are looking for relationships that are reliable, dependable, sure – those that will guard our affections and our hurts. Have you found this trusting relationship in your church family?

Not many of us can say that we are experiencing a deep trusting relationship. I am speaking for myself. I have lived for many years and have never really learned to trust anyone. People have let me down and have been careless in dealing with my emotions. I have been angered by such behaviors. And now I find it difficult to trust anyone. In the not too distant past, I decided to try the "trusting" idea because I had heard that trusting was a good experience. I was told that there was reason to trust, it was safe. No, I soon learned that I was not safe. And again I learned that "Safety" is more than mere words. It is not safe just because one says, "Trust me, I am safe." It is hard to find a safe person or safe place. But it is worth pursuing, for there is safety out there. It is for us to find, with God's help. Please believe me, when it is found, our world will be different, it will become the planet we have been waiting for. Then I wonder, does the fact that I do not trust anyone affect how much I trust myself and even God?

If I do not trust myself, I will not trust others. I have learned that trust entices trust. When I trust to you my heart and emotions, you tend to trust your heart to me. It is simple, I trust you, and you trust me. If I do not trust you, I will not tell you those things dear to my heart that are really hurting me. Neither will you share with me your secrets. This is fair. Consequently, I will never become close to you and you to me. We will never know of each other's real joy or real pain. Therefore closeness and intimacy will never be shared by us. There may never be a community, and when there is no community, we remain in our own fake worlds, hiding in our confined closets, complaining that our world is too restrictive and cold.

Sometimes, we blame the world for our problems, without realizing that our problems have to do with our level of trust. Whom do we trust, and how much of ourselves are we prepared to entrust to others? I will tell you one more time, I have not done well in trusting others. Then I wonder, since I as a pastor have failed to model the meaning of trust, could this influence my church family? If the pastor does not trust his church family, will the church family trusts the pastor and one another? While I confess, that I have not opened my secrets to my church family, I must also reveal that whenever I cautiously let someone into my life and disclose that I am a human being, that someone appreciates me more and tends to gravitate closer to me. I am still learning how to trust, how to build community and make the church a ***Safe, Sweet Home***.

I am also learning that trust building is heart building. As we open our hearts, we are building trust and are reaching deep into one's inner closet and viewing privileged information. This calls for tenderness, perceptiveness and patience. Never should we betray the heart that has been opened to our care. Rather, let us handle it with loving, padded care. Let us provide for it a ***Safe, Sweet Home***. Let it feel warm, comfortable and cozy and we will have developed a friendship forever and for God's kingdom.

> Do others feel safe around me?
> Can I be trusted to carry someone's heart?

This subject of trust is vital to the life of the church. From my studies and personal experience, it is apparent that where there is trust, we grow spiritually and emotionally, and the church grows numerically. Why? Because where there is trust, we are free to become ourselves. We feel free to trust our hearts to others. We are freed of the burdensome baggage we often carry. It is true that trust is not as natural as breathing. Neither is it as sudden as the next moment. No, trust is earned and may be the result of a long tedious journey. But when it is born, a new life begins, and one soon finds that it has been worth the waiting and the journey. If you are enjoying a trusting relationship, please continue to cherish and nurture it.

If you trust no one and no one trusts you, let me encourage you to search until the Lord leads you into a trusting relationship. Find someone you can trust and who will trust you. Gradually open the doors to who you really are. Let him know that you have a name, but you also have a heart. Allow yourself to flow out and allow others to see the real you. Let your tears flow. Tell him that you are hurting. Invite him to pray for your children who may be still fighting against God. Tell him that you are very uncomfortable about going to the hospital. Just open your heart. It will feel good. And encourage others to experience the same. And soon, we will be citizens of a trusting family.

My challenge is for us to become intentional advocates for making our churches a ***Safe, Sweet Home***, a place where God lives in delight and we His children are so much in love that the radiance of Jesus and the Holy Spirit are breaking through the walls to clasp hands with the community of seekers. Let us begin to talk intentionally about what contributions each one can make towards creating a church which is a ***Safe, Sweet Home***. And please, please let us not rest, until our church family feels safe and the one who visits our church feels safe, as safe as Jesus feels.

As I was sifting through a pile of my wife's papers, I encountered these words, which failed to identify the author. The title of the writing is:

Creating Christ's Holy Atmosphere

"All growing Christian churches have one thing in common. They have a positive, safe and joyous atmosphere. They may be conservative or liberal, traditional or progressive, wealthy or poor, small or large. However, without a surrounding influence of trust, the emotional effect of all other attributes will come to naught. This cannot be compromised. The study of and spiritual embodiment of the life and ministry of Jesus Christ will provide all that is necessary to obtain this holy effect."

I have, in these few pages, invited us to keep the atmosphere of our church family ***Safe and Sweet***, that we will become intentional in affecting change where there are unresolved emotional and social issues. Time is short. Jesus is soon to come. Let us attract our people to come home, to remain home in the church family where it is ***Safe and Sweet***.

As God nurtured the children of Israel to be the spectacle for its culture, so God has planted the church family and us Christians to be healing pools for our dry, thirsty, troubled society. We are a lighthouse. We are a harbor. We are a bridge. It is to the church family and to us Christians that

God sends His children to find a ***Safe, Sweet Home***. Here our burdens rest, our turmoil cease, our hearts are warmed, we find friends, and we can smile again, for we are **SAFE**.

May the Lord build a people, and a church,
that inspires trust, safety, and sweetness
that welcomes diversity, challenges,
opportunities,
and a God clothed with humanity.

Reflection Page

- Do you feel that your home, work place or church is a safe place?
- What factors make it safe?

____

____

- What factors make it unsafe?

____

____

- From your experience, what factors may contribute to making you feel safe?

____

____

- With whom do you feel safe?

____

____

- How important to you is the subject of safety?

____

____

Chapter 7

Growing Towards Each Other

Great results and great answers spring from great questions.

Growing Towards Each Other is about understanding people and how I feel and relate to them. I may not be able to change others, but I can choose to change myself. In this section are some questions. They are constructed to make you feel that you and another are in conversation or you are addressing yourself. The questions allow you to examine why you do the things you do and help you to develop a deeper acceptance of others.

These questions, when appropriately responded to, will bring you closer to another and build a stronger, positive relationship. And isn't this what we desire as we live and walk with others? I have placed these questions in categories. Some are to be examined by yourself and some together with the person with whom you want to grow.

Looking at Me –

- Am I comfortable opening my heart to you?
- What about you do I like and want to emulate?

- ➢ What might you talk about that would make me afraid, and why would I be afraid?
- ➢ What do I appreciate most about you?
- ➢ What do you like to talk to me about that would make me sad?
- ➢ What is it that you do or say that makes me happy?
- ➢ What do I enjoy talking to you about?
- ➢ What do I have that I would like to share with you because I care about you?
- ➢ Do I feel that you will accept me, regardless of how many times I have failed you?

Dealing with Me

- ➢ What can I do to make you feel comfortable around me?
- ➢ Is there anything that I can give you more of and if so, what?
- ➢ What do I need to change so that I can better understand and relate to you?
- ➢ What can I do to communicate more openly and honestly?

Considering You

- ➢ What word or words best describe how I feel about you?
- ➢ If I were to write a book about you, what would I name it?
- ➢ What pleasant memories do I have of our times together?
- ➢ How is my life impacted by you?

Looking at Us

- ➢ Why do I want you as a friend?

- What in our relationship am I most thankful for?
- How much do I enjoy your presence?
- Do I desire our friendship to grow?
- Would I move into your neighborhood, or even next door to you?
- When I am feeling lonesome, do I long for your company?
- When I am feeling good, what do I want to tell you?
- When I am successful or sad, do I want to tell you?

> "Lord, teach me to trust you that I may trust others and others may trust me."

Looking at Our Friendship

- How much do I respect you or you me?
- How important is forgiveness in our relationship?
- Do I feel that you really want to hear what I have to say?
- Has there been a time when you were in difficulty and I came to your aid?
- If you and I went on a vacation, would it be a delight or a disaster?

Caring for Us

- How often do you want me to tell you that you are special to me?
- When you are unhappy with me, how do you want me to respond to you?

- While talking with you at the beginning of the work week, what would I say that would encourage you?
- What things can we do together which might excite us?

Growing Our Friendship

- How important to you is my friendship?
- What things do I need to share with you?
- What makes you feel appreciative of me?
- What is it that I do or say that tends to separate us?
- Do you sometimes, in my absence, think of me in a positive way?
- Have I ever made you feel special?
- How would I best demonstrate my caring love for you?
- Are we closer now than we were? Why?

Plant a tree and watch it grow Create a friendship and watch life flow.

Reflection Page

- How do you plan to apply the questions in this chapter?

- Is there someone with whom you would like to share these questions?

- If you had the opportunity, what questions would you like to ask the author or concerns you would like to discuss?

- What questions would you add to this chapter?

Chapter 8

Making it Clean

"Timely advice is as lovely as golden apples in a silver basket." Proverbs 25:11.

A church member and I were in conversation, and I attempted to be kind in my verbal delivery. Our time together concluded, and I thought we separated with good feelings. A few days later, I received a telephone call from her. She desired to have another meeting with me, and so we did. At this meeting, she recaptured our previous conversation. She indicated that she had been reflecting on my statements and was offended. She had come to tell me that she was hurt and wanted to straighten things out. This was my opportunity to apologize and I did. She was satisfied. She indicated that what she wanted was to make it clean and that she would not talk about it to anyone else, only me. So I complimented her for coming to me and me only. We separated, smiling and in good spirits.

Making it Clean means clearing the debris that causes relationships to become murky, clearing the hard feelings between individuals, and making wrongs right. It is neither easy nor natural to make it clean. And yet it is the God-like thing to do. At the very time of writing this book, my own heart was concerned about a misunderstanding between a church member and me. It was not a major concern, but a concern that troubled me. I knew that some cleaning needed to happen. Who else was better to initiate the cleaning, but me? Oh, how I was fearful. So I walked up to the Lord and prayed for strength and wisdom. And even after praying, I still did not receive an electric shock, empowering me to go ahead. But before I made that fearful call, notice what I did – I telephoned an individual who I knew would share some pleasantries with me. After this call, I slowly and fearfully made the call to the church member with whom I needed to make things clean. The phone rang, and I hoped no one was home, but suddenly there was a cheery voice, and I utilized the cheery moment to buy time.

The moment came. Yes, I explained that I had called to revisit the misunderstanding between us. And from here, the conversation was pleasant, objective and warm. I apologized and so did she. Apologies were like sweet roses, and when we concluded our time together, we were both laughing and feeling good. It was not easy to walk into, but once completed, it felt good. ***Making it Clean*** can be a joyous, fruitful experience if the parties involved have the right attitude – to build peace, togetherness and friendship.

As you know very well, the best chance for a reasonably good working relationship is when you are working alone. When one or more individuals are added to your space, the opportunities for elevated stresses increase. And so when I walked into the working space of Lester, it soon became clear that we were headed for collision. It was not because we disliked each other, not at all. It was because we were different individuals with different values and saw things differently. We had not talked about how to cultivate a good working relationship. We avoided the issue and worked as professionals. One day, someone saw what was happening between two Christian professionals and suggested that there should be a carefrontation, i.e. a meeting of our minds in a caring and safe environment, where we could express ourselves and still be friends. I thought about this and was afraid since I had never done this before. But after processing the alternatives, I decided that a carefrontation was the right thing to do.

Other parties were involved, so they were all called and a meeting was scheduled. Was I afraid of this moment? Yes. But was it the right thing to do? Surely. This is how I prepared myself, I wrote all my concerns and planned to read them. Once I prepared this document, and re-visited it, I became more relaxed. Then I made two copies, one for me and the other for Lester. Walking into that meeting was a stressful moment, but I would not forget what to say nor be misquoted, for the document would be my faithful partner. My emotions would not climb away from me, nor my memory run away. I could depend on my document.

Do we always need a written document? No. But there might be times when it is very useful. This was a very good meeting. There was clarity and understanding between all the parties. And now life could go on. After this carefrontation meeting, I became more convinced that when individuals do experience misunderstandings and just cannot get along, this is the time to come together to talk, to clarify and live in the beauty of Christian love.

Because of meeting, talking and clarifying these misunderstandings with my friend, I left the meeting with a sense of peace and goodwill. I felt good. I was glad that it happened. And since it was so beneficial to all parties, I have likened that meeting to coming to a flower garden. A flower garden is the home of beauty and peace. Often troubled hearts visit a flower garden for the meal of peace and renewal. Likewise if you are troubled because of an unresolved relationship, then it is time to come to the garden, the carefrontation meeting, the meeting of minds in an environment where it is safe and misunderstandings can be resolved.

Dorothy and Evelyn were involved in a conversation. Both parties were hot and neither was listening nor understanding. So naturally, in the heat of the moment, both separated with hurting hearts. Nothing was resolved. I observed Dorothy as she grieved at the way the conversation went. About a quarter of a mile away, Evelyn sat under her roof, silent and fuming. She knew that Dorothy was wrong for not understanding her and acting so contrary to good judgment. She would not talk with Dorothy. She was too angry. But some time later that day, I witnessed these individuals come to the garden of peace. There, Dorothy took responsibility for her behavior, apologized and asked for forgiveness. Evelyn likewise responded. They cried together. They hugged. They separated in peace and love and hoped to be friends. There are not many sights more beautiful than this. This is why I liken this experience to a flower garden.

A church member, Lesmine, told me this: Lester was in conversation with a friend of hers and told her to be careful about choosing Lesmine as a friend. This friend did not like this conversation, and so she told Lesmine about it. Lesmine became upset and was undecided about what to do with this information. After a few days, she met Lester at church and said to him, "Can I talk to you for a second? I want to talk to you about something. It has been bothering me and I am going to be mad at myself if I don't handle it. I have to be honest with you. Why did you say that about me?" Lester paused and then explained why. Lesmine then asked, "If you are my friend and you thought that I was handling myself inappropriately and I needed lots of prayers, then why didn't you pick up the phone and call me?" Lester replied, "I probably should have, and I am sorry that I didn't." Let us lift our hats to Lesmine for carefronting Lester and to Lester for apologizing.

How is the above situation usually handled? Lesmine who was upset would continue to be upset. During this time she would discuss the situation with several individuals who had no business to know. She would express her anger and maybe seek for ways to get even with Lester by sharing inflammatory information about him. She may avoid contacts with him that may lead to breaking a friendship. And what does this do for a community? It fragments. How nice it is when individuals come together to reconcile as did Lester and Lesmine.

When two individuals come together to make wrongs right, this is not the time to discuss or prove who is right or wrong. If rightness or wrongness is important at this time, it is possible that you are not sorry for the wrong done and are not ready to make it right. It is appropriate to come to this meeting with the attitude that you are the party who has done wrong. Then, accept that you were wrong. Accept that you misunderstood what you heard. Accept that you were wrong for sharing the information with others rather than clarifying it with the source. Accept that you lost control of yourself. Do not blame anyone. Simply accept responsibility.

After you have accepted in your mind that you were wrong, you are now more ready to express it. You will be able to say it and mean it. For what good is it to say you are sorry if within your heart you are not? I suggest that words without feeling or conviction are fruitless. Saying with conviction that you are sorry will leave you feeling humbled and small. Most of us take pride in knowing that we are most times right and hate to accept our errors, but to accept our wrongness, though humbling, will leave us feeling gratified.

Now when we talk about ***Making it Clean*** am I asking you to awake the sleeping giant? Am I asking you to dig for some past, settled hurts, just because you feel disturbed by them? Not necessarily so. This is not a call to empty the trash can hoping to find sad memories, memories of people you might have caused hurt, instead this is a call for you to ask Jesus to bring instances to mind that you need to make right. Sometimes we perceived hurts where there were none. The hurt was in our minds. Therefore, do not stir up a sleeping giant or make a mountain out of a mole hill.

And who goes first? When there has been a misunderstanding between two individuals and there needs to be a resolution, who goes first? Who takes the initiative, who makes the first contact? The answer from the Bible:

> ***"So if you are standing before the altar in the temple, offering a sacrifice to God, and you suddenly remember that someone has something against you, leave your sacrifice there beside the altar. Go and be reconciled to that person. Then come and offer your sacrifice to God." Matthew 5:23, 24.***

This scripture suggests that you have caused someone to hurt, you have done wrong, and for this reason, this person has mixed feelings towards you. ***"Someone has something against you."*** Then it becomes your privilege to take the initiative to go and make it right. You might not be sure about the wrong you did, but you are to go and make it right anyway.

> ***"If another believer sins against you, go privately and point out the fault…." Matthew 18:15.***

This scripture suggests that if someone has done you wrong and has hurt you, then it becomes your privilege to take the initiative to go to that person. Together identify the wrong and make it right. So whether someone did you wrong or you did someone wrong, your call is to go and make it right. There is to be no sitting back, waiting to see who goes first. You go first. So for us church people, the call of Jesus is this: before meeting for worship each week, is for us to examine our human relations with family, friends, work-mates and others, to see if we are actually ready to worship Him. And if not, take care of business immediately. God frowns on acts of worship where hearts are cluttered with unresolved matters.

In the remaining section of this chapter, please allow me to dedicate to you some thoughts, which if tried, will provide you a good chance of experiencing satisfaction in the process of ***Making it Clean***. I am suggesting that you experience or practice the following before you make it clean:

1. **Be Restful** – Before Lester faces a potential employer for an important job interview, one that means much to him, he takes time to prepare himself physically and emotionally. He cleans himself up, dresses appropriately and makes sure

he is rested and mentally refreshed. He wants his mind to be fresh and clear. Likewise when we are coming face to face to make it clean, we will be better prepared if we are feeling good about ourselves, our dress, our mental attitude and restfulness. A reconciliatory meeting might not bring about the best results if it happens just after work or during work time when minds are taxed and tired. So make an appointment for a time when the parties involved can be prepared. Make it a special date. It is worth it.

2. **Be Prayerful** – There is nothing the Christian can accomplish without the blessings and presence of our Lord. And as sinful humanity, we know that the greater the task, the greater the need for prayer. When a family member is diagnosed with a terminal illness, prayer requests are broadcast across a large geographical area. Many and continual prayers are needed, and we do this well. We will continue praying until there is a finality of some kind. Mending a broken heart is a mighty task. And where possible, a team of prayer warriors should be praying for this meeting. Surely, the parties themselves should be the most active in praying before and during the meeting. If the meeting is progressing smoothly, praise the Lord for the progress, and if resolution seems far away, it is appropriate to stop and pray. It is known that prayers offered during meetings change the course of events. It is difficult to continue to be indifferent to each other while talking to God about love and unity. So pray and pray and praise the Lord.

3. **Be Reconciliatory** – Often the result of a venture is largely dependent upon what we invested into it. What you put into it is what you get out. Why do we come face to face with the one who has wronged us? Isn't it for the purpose of admitting, confessing, forgiving and loving? Basically, we come face to face with the one who has wronged us to make wrongs right, and to plant seeds that will grow into peace fruits. This means that before the meeting you inform yourself that this meeting will be a good thing. Everything

will be all right. No matter what happens, no matter how Lester behaves, you will not lose your temper. You will retain a Christian posture for which you and the Lord will be well pleased. You see, being at peace with Lester is very important to you, the community and the Lord. What do you suppose would happen if we all faced our next meeting with the one who had wronged us with that attitude? I am encouraging you to try. You might like the result.

4. **Be Open** – This is not easy. Most of us know what has happened in the past and what will happen in the present and future. And such knowledge acts as a shut-off valve for further development. Therefore, is it easy to come to this meeting with a closed mind? Yes! I have learned over the years that the human mind, closed, is not easily penetrable by words, but by wind, storm and fire. It takes the power of the Lord to change our minds and to allow us to see as He sees. Therefore, it is well for us to pray for an open mind.

   This does not mean forgetting the past, rather it is not allowing your present to be controlled by the past. It means giving the Lord of love and grace an opportunity to speak to your heart as you intend to blend with another. In my thoughts, the one who is open is the one who has committed himself to be a keen listener.

   In this meeting, one of the objectives is to listen to what is being said. Show that what is being said is important and well received. Encourage the other person to talk. And do not be damaged by the flow of volcanic substances that may flow from those talking lips, for from these same lips will soon flow soft, jelly-like delicacies. In my thoughts, the one who is open is the one who has committed himself or herself to understand the moment and the experience. Often, misunderstanding is the reason for conflicts. One intended to convey one thing. The observer or receiver saw it differently and responded differently.

   Truly, not many of us think alike, even though we work closely. There has to be a constant conscious effort to understand what is being said or done. This means listening to understand. And when the message is unclear, then it is time to ask questions for clarification. I have found it satisfying when I have taken time for clarification. So, remember to listen, and then listen and listen again. And try to listen from your heart and not just your head. This might bring the true story to you.

In my thoughts, the one who has an open mind is the one who has committed himself to be accepting. Even though you may not agree with what the other party does or says, you are willing to accept him as a unique gift of God. He was lovingly created by God and has been sustained by God for a specific purpose. God loves him, accepts him and in God's mind, he is fine. Then who am I to change him? Who are you to change him? The obvious position, then, is to accept him and praise God for him. Affirm his gifts and seek to compliment him and his gifts. It is so marvelous to work together in unity with God's children even though we are different. It is even more marvelous how God works with us and includes us all into His plan, even though we are all different.

5. **Be Kind** – This maybe could summarize all that I have said thus far or will say. It is so very important to be kind. In fact, you will agree that kindness goes beyond making it clean. Kindness is the essence and perfume of living. Kindness kills the enemy and makes friends. Everyone appreciates kindness. While we forget many other great events of life, we will remember kindness. When I revisit my past, what usually surface are the people and events that meant "kindness" to me. Those who are dearest to me are those who have been the kindest to me. I hope that by now you are impressed with the fact that kindness is a key to be used in the process of ***Making it Clean***.

   What do I mean by "kind"? I mean, please approach Lester with a gentle heart. Seek to heal his wounds. Already he is hurting and needs no further wounds or hurt. Treat him just as you would desire to be treated. Leave all the mean, cutting words behind. Even if Lester is rude, vindictive and condemnatory, do not return to him the same favor. For Jesus' sake, offer him kind words and looks seasoned with smiles. Sometimes we are stretched thin and find it difficult to be kind in these situations. At these times, call upon Jesus, take a deep breath, break from talking and then reconvene. When the meeting is over, may it be said of you, "She was so kind to me." It is my sense that in the process of ***Making it Clean***, it is not important who wins or who is right. But it is utterly important how kind the individuals are to each other. Kindness will make friends when other ways may not.

> It is better to be kind than right.
>
> It is better to be thoughtful than thorough.
>
> It is better to be sensitive than straightforward.
>
> It is better to admit wrong than demand right.

Someday people may say of you –

> "He was a good teacher,"
>
> "He was a good pastor,"
>
> "He was a good athlete,"
>
> "He dressed well,"
>
> "He was very healthy because he ate well,"
>
> "He was intelligent."

But will they also say of you or me–

> "He was so kind and gentle in his dealings with people."

6. **Be Forgiving** – This idea of forgiving is complex. I have not fully understood the God-like definition of forgiveness. Let us concentrate on what happens after we have met with the one who did us wrong. We came mentally and physically prepared. We came in a prayerful and reconciliatory mode. We came with an open mind, which

allowed us to listen, understand and accept. After all this, surely the grace and love of God would have been pouring down upon us and binding us to the one who had previously wronged us. We now find ourselves loving and desiring to become one with him. We are sorry that ill feelings once burned between us, and we desire to live together in peace and love forever. And you know that life will be different between you and Lester. You will stand to defend him. You will pray for him daily and even long to be in his presence and enjoy it. When all these are true for you, then you know that you have offered to Lester, by God's grace, forgiveness. You have forgiven him. Praise God.

7. **Be Language Smart** – As we attempt to clean up the misunderstandings between us, there will be times when finding the correct language may be difficult. There may be times when we will never find it. For whatever language we use, the other person will be distressed.

   I clearly remember when my best language was not good enough. I was only seven years of age, living in Jamaica. My dear aunt found it necessary to discuss with me her findings about my childhood pranks. However, her information was not according to my recollection, and I desired to correct her. If it had been one of my peers who had presented that false information, I would have said: "You are a liar." But to my aunt, different words were required. So after diligent thought, it finally came from my lips with deep respect for her, "You are telling a lie right there." This was my best language. This should have worked. But no, it did not. For my aunt thought this was very disrespectful and took after me to administer justice with a stinging stick, but I flew from her presence. She soon found my mother and registered how disrespectful I was.

   Sometimes, our best language will still tie us to trouble. However, it is still right to pray and ponder, "What words will bring the best results?" Words have different meanings to different individuals at different times. And there are times when one's emotional and physical state will determine how one relates to words. Therefore it does make good sense that I would give serious consideration to the words that I plan to use.

Think of the young man who is in love and plans to meet his girlfriend for an evening. Does he not give thought to what he would say to her in order to receive the best response? Or if he were planning to ask her to marry him, would he not even write it to ensure that he said the right words? Or if you were going for a job interview, would you not give consideration to what you would say? As I meet with Lester to make clean our misunderstandings, I will by the wisdom of the Lord, desire to use words which will attract togetherness and harmony and not divide nor generate hostility. I will not accuse Lester using language such as, "You were the one who started this problem." Or, "I think you are the one to be blamed." It seems more uniting when I say, "It is unclear to me how this all happened, but it is clear that I have played a part in this misunderstanding and I am sorry. Will you please forgive me?" The language we use is an enemy or a friend. Therefore, please use it wisely and in a friendly manner. It will bring friendly results.

8. **Be Timely** – Is it important to you to make clean the misunderstandings between you and Lester? Then consider it important enough to create an environment conducive for the best results possible. Now, consider this: We usually visit a doctor when we are sick and or in pain. We rush in to see the principal about our child when the school has done wrong. We confront our spouses when they have done something to upset our emotions. It seems that we are motivated to act when we are emotionally hot. True? Well, experience has taught me that timing is very important when I am thinking of ***Making it Clean*** with Lester. To run into him after church may not provide the best scenario. To introduce the subject at the end of the day, immediately after a fatiguing day at work may be a very poor choice. I am not

sure which is the best time for ***Making it Clean***, but please allow me to suggest an approach. This is what I would like to do – I will call Lester on the telephone or speak to him face to face, saying:

> "Lester, there is a very important matter that I need to resolve, and you are an important person in helping me to resolve this. I desire to establish a meeting time with you. I will be available on Friday evening at 7:30 or on Sunday at 2:00 p.m. Can you be available one of these times?"

Please notice that I offered Lester choices. These times that I have suggested are times that I believe will provide minimum hardships. Hopefully, they will be times when both of us will be emotionally and physically rested. Should Lester desire to know the reason for our meeting, I will briefly share with him the reason. I will share with him that three months ago, there was a misunderstanding between us and it has bothered me ever since. I will also share with him that I need to resolve this and that he is the one to assist me. This information may reduce Lester's anxieties and prepare him for the meeting.

Privacy is important. Most people would prefer a carefrontation in private. So make sure that you provide this. A convenient place for this meeting may be in a room in the church, a restaurant, a home that is quiet, in your office at work, or in your car. You may be visible to others, but your conversation should be confined between you two only. Remember to respect the privacy of the moment. Another great idea is to conclude the meeting with prayer, praise and affirmation. Perhaps you could set a time to have a meal together. And let this be a time for celebration. This would work well for me, and I hope for you.

9. **Be Gummy** – Gum sticks. It is difficult to rid yourself of gum. Gum wants to stay with you, whether you want it to or not. In your consideration of ***Making it Clean***, there might come the time when it will be convenient to run away

thinking, "This whole thing is too hard. It is not worth all the bother." So in response you say: "I am fine. I am not upset." And you walk away. Walking away suggests that you are not fine. All is not well. Saying that you are fine is simply a pacifier, to get the other party off your back in order that you will be free to stew and steam some more. I plead with you not to take the easy road. Do not walk away from the situation unresolved. Why? Because pain is painful. And pain tends to linger. Life is too short and precious to be stained with pain and torment. So please distribute a dose of peace and contentment by sticking with the situation until it is satisfactorily resolved. Think of the benefits that may be obtained from this.

There may be a time when you need to take a break from the situation. At such time, it will be appropriate to say, "I am not feeling good about this conversation at this moment. Give me a little time and I will get back to you." Then take this time out to process, but be sure to come back. Be honest with yourself and the person involved. Walk, talk and live how you really feel. Only remember to do it with tenderness.

Now that we have spent this time talking about ***Making it Clean***, an important question should begin to stir your mind. "What kinds of situations do I need to make clean and how far back should I go?" This section of the book takes the position that this question has no definitive answer. Several factors are to be considered. This book also takes the position that not everything has to be made clean. We may not need to contact everyone since childhood for the purpose of making wrongs right. Let me illustrate - I was just about sixteen years of age when I stopped attending church. I clearly remember the two events which drove me away. I was away from home attending high school when the first one occurred. Even though I was away from home, church was still important to me, so I rode my bicycle to church. This was my only means of transportation. As I rode onto the church grounds, two deacons met me and chastised me for riding my bike onto the church grounds. Their approach was crude, and I had no time for them, so I rode away on my bike and never returned to that church or any other church for a period of time.

The other occurred some months later. I maybe would have gone to church at my home town, but while visiting home, during vacation, I met one of the church leaders. He knew that I was no longer attending church. Though I was glad to meet him, he was cold to me. Previously, he would have greeted me warmly and addressed me as "Brother Brown." This was an inside name. I enjoyed that name. It meant that I belonged. But on this day, he addressed me, using another name, thus telling me that I no longer belonged to the church family. On this day, it was sealed in my mind that church was not the place for me. Now, my question is this: after these many years, must I fly, telephone or write to Jamaica, seeking these individuals for the purpose of ***Making it Clean***? It is clear in my mind that the Lord is not asking me to do this. These men might have done me wrong, or I might have over reacted to their behaviors. And if I conclude that they did me wrong, I will ask the Lord to forgive them and forgive my selfish responses.

Because an individual chews gum in church, which disturbs you, does not mean that the individual had offended you. It may simply mean that you have a problem with gum chewing in church. The problem is with you, not the one chewing the gum. And the way to change that is to sit where the gum chewer is not visible to you. On the other hand, if you are displeased with your church sister chewing gum in church and you begin a campaign by involving others, hoping to distort her character, then you have wronged her and need to ***Make it Clean***. You need to apologize and stop.

It is my compelling conviction that the time is now to make clean those unresolved, breaking, hurting feelings fuming between us, those feelings which hold us as prisoners and affect growth, function and relationship building. It is my compelling conviction, that for too long, many of us have been hiding behind a mask, pretending that all is well. But the pain inside reminds us that all is not well. When your heart is troubled, when worship, spirituality and health are affected, when you cannot look into the individual's face with a warm smile and say "Hello", and mean it from your heart, then it is time to ***Make it Clean***. And when the individuals are within reach, by telephone, letter, e-mail or face to face, then you can ***Make it Clean*** personally. And when none of these is available, you might do the next best, ***Make it Clean*** through Jesus. Ask Jesus to present your request for forgiveness to God the Father. This works well for me, and I hope it will work for you.

Are there cases where ***Making it Clean*** is a challenge or impossibility? Yes. The other party or parties might be uncooperative. Death might have occurred. Relationships might be worsened. The timing might not be right. And there might be other reasons. Then you and God will be the judge. But whatever you do, remember to do this: complete the process of ***Making it Clean.*** Work until it is totally clean. Do not run away. Please.

This discussion may not be popular, though very Biblical. My earlier years were devoid of this subject. No one invited me to enter this peace-making, peace-loving, wonder-working world. But here in my last years, this invitation and opportunity have come to me, and this I cherish. For you, this might be a new journey. But it is the high and right journey. It is the Christ-like journey. If you have never walked it, then begin to walk it, please. If you are walking it, keep walking, please.

Now that we have spent time on this challenging subject of ***Making it Clean***, let us break with a few personal questions:

- Has there been a misunderstanding between you and an individual?
- How long has this misunderstanding kept you apart?
- Has this misunderstanding been resolved?
- Has this book given you a desire to resolve it?
- Do you know of others in your church or family who need to ***Make it Clean***?

- Do you believe your community, church, home or workplace would be a better place if individuals would come forward and ***Make it Clean***?
- Are you willing, by God's wisdom, to tell others of the freedom that you experienced from ***Making it Clean***?

Who will you tell?
When will you tell?

Oh God, please enter our church.
Oh God, please enter me.
Cause us to hunger and thirst after oneness,
understanding and tenderness.
Fill us with your eyes, ears and heart.
Cause us to bend in humility and love,
And make us one.

> What the church does not do is left for me to do.
> For the call of God is not for the church, but for me.

Reflection Page

- Discuss how you feel about accepting the fact that you have been wrong.

- Is it difficult for you to apologize? And if yes, why?

- Some individuals may choose to deal with an issue while others may choose to avoid it. What is more comfortable for you and why?

- Discuss what you thought was the main points in this chapter. Why were they important to you?

- What changes may occur after individuals have been to the flower garden and conflicts have been resolved?

  a.____

  b.____

  c.____

Chapter 9

Bitter and Sweet

The view once seen as unlovely may be transformed into a botanical garden.

When you left your home for the office, you prayed to your Father, God. You told Him how you loved Him. You committed your life to Him and requested that His presence would stay beside you to comfort you and to guide all that you would do that day, including your relationship with others and how you would deal with them. And yet, so often, something happens, and we forget that for which we prayed. We forget that we had requested that God would deal with others through us. And so we advance on our own and spoil God's plans. We take things into our own hands and deal with others according to our plans. And that is when the human relation battles begin. That is when hearts are pierced and pained.

I have lived for many years and have few memories of intentionally hurting anyone. I have most times attempted to care for the feelings of others, though surely, I have said and done things that have caused hurt. And when I was aware of such hurting effects, what did I do? I went along with life and hoped that time would have healed the hurt so that I would no longer have to deal with it. Time should have healed the hurt. But maybe time has not. So what must I do? What would you do? Truly, I have always been a coward and frightened to carefront difficult, challenging situations. Therefore I avoided carefrontations, even though the Bible calls Christians to this task. Instead of carefronting, and being freed, we avoid the conflict and become imprisoned by it.

Some of the reasons we avoid the conflict could be because we are afraid of the pain, the other party will not cooperate, we do not care, or we do not know how. But whatever the reason, we walk on the avoidance track. So the conflict and its consequences continue. We carry them in our chest, like lead bullets. And for some of us, this stops life. Recently, a church member told me that she was trapped by her conflict. She did not know what to do. She needed help. "I want to go on with my life, but I cannot." she said. Personally, I am learning that it is important to deal with conflicts for, where it is not given attention, life may be halted and handicapped.

In the case of this church member, she was willing to resolve the conflict, but the other person would not cooperate. Well, this might be the time for her to resolve the conflict by herself. She might need to tell herself that she has done everything possible. There is nothing more she can do. She must now consider the case closed and leave the rest to God. Dismiss every taunting memory of the situation, pray for the peace of Jesus, and go on with her life. The fact that the other party avoided the conflict brought more hardship to the church member, but God can bring peace.

Today, I am thankful to my partner in ministry, Gary Parks. When we began ministry together a few years ago, he shared with me one of his passions, which is this: When there is a strained relationship between church members or family members, one should take the responsibility to reconcile. Gary encouraged me to experience this for myself, for he knew that I was dealing with some issues. He said he was not pushing me if I were uncomfortable. And yes, I was uncomfortable, for I had never done this in my pastoral nor adult life. But I realized that reconciliation was the Christian thing to do. Praise God for the courage, for I did it. It was good for all parties involved. There was clarity. There was a new direction. There was an opening to hearts. And now, because of experiencing this, it has become much easier to come face to face with others and say, "I am sorry for hurting you by the things I said about you. I should not have done this. I promise not to do this again by God's help. Will you please forgive me?" Praise God, He has enabled me to do this with Gary's encouragement.

On another occasion, four of us met in Gary's office to clarify some issues. It was great having Gary there to lead us. He informed us that it was not necessary to discuss the issues or who was wrong, but that what was important was that we take responsibility for what we had done and apologize. It was like heavenly music hearing each one saying: "I am sorry, will you please forgive me?" "I forgive you." I never thought this could happen. But it did, and we all left the office with a heavenly spirit. Had we not come face to face to apologize and become one, just think of how different our attitudes towards one another would have been. Praise God for that opportunity. Apologizing is surely not the human thing to do, but it is the God-like, Christ-like, and moral thing to do.

Now, may I ask a simple question? Have you hurt someone and need to experience the joy and victory from apologizing? Or do you know of someone who has hurt you and needs to experience the same? It is my guess that there are many Christians and many family members who need to be in a similar room, like I was, to experience God re-creating His character and joy among His family. Today, I am pleading with you to release yourself from bondage. Set yourself free. Apologize, be friends, be Christian and begin to live again. Experience sweetness, for sweetness comes after apologizing and becoming one again.

Recently I was able to liken apologizing to mowing my lawn the wrong way. For years I mowed my lawn going the same direction, and it seemed that my mower knew the way and easily, smoothly sailed along. The grass, in its attempt to cooperate with the mower, laid flat in a direction to facilitate the mowing process. One day, my wife noted that tracks were being formed from my following the same course and requested that I mow going the opposite direction. I obeyed and tried, only to return to my old ways. Why? Mowing the opposite direction was different. For me, the opposite direction was unnatural and therefore difficult. So is apologizing to someone whom we have wronged and hurt. Though not humanly natural, it is the God-like thing to do.

Recently, I had the invitation to come face to face with someone whom I had wronged. It was a troubling invitation. My thoughts were multiple. Why should I apologize? Should I not defend myself? Will it not make me feel small to apologize? How could I acknowledge that I was not perfect and had done wrong, since I am a pastor? Wouldn't it be nice if the appointment were cancelled? But my Christian conviction surmounted these thoughts and, I came face to face with the moment. Listen, once the moment had come and attitudes and hearts were humbled and surrendered to the Holy Spirit, then the joy of the Lord began to flow. It was a moment of courage, humility and fear. But it was also a moment of joy and victory. It sounded like music to hear the words falling from my lips: "I am sorry for.... Will you please forgive me?" It was more melodious, hearing the sound from across the room, "Yes, I forgive you." Then we prayed and hugged each other and left as friends. And God rejoiced because He had won the battle. You should have been in that room to experience the power of Jesus. You would have known that there was a spirit of reconciliation and the presence of God. There were tears and pain, but they all melted away into joy.

Again, apologizing is surely not the human thing to do. But it is the God-like, Christ-like, moral thing to do.

If today you are experiencing a distorted relationship with someone and you know that you are partially or fully responsible, please prayerfully, humbly step forward and offer your apologies. Or, like the Bible directs: if you know that someone has a problem with you, even though you are innocent, walk over and make it right. Please note that the idea is not to go and defend yourself. Not at all. The call is to walk over, simply and prayerfully say, "Lester, I am sorry for offending you yesterday. I know that I did hurt you. I am sorry and I promise not to do it again, by God's help. Will you please forgive me?" Then wait for an answer. And now watch God work miracles and be prepared to be a part of it.

Since I had the opportunity to apologize for wrongs that I did, I am more appreciative of the benefits of apologizing. And I desire to share with you what benefits I have received, what sweetness has refreshed my life. I have learned from experience that an apology is these things:

- The parent of good fortune and future,
- Heaven's human gift,
- A ladder to greatness and the aroma of humility,
- A ruler which measures how tall or short one is,
- A friend,
- A call to oneness,
- The beginning of a prayer life and the bud of a radiant morning,
- The entrance to rest and renewal,
- Servant-hood, not slavery,
- A door, not a covering,
- For the strong and brave, not the weak and coward.

You too, can experience these and more if only you will allow the Lord to enable you to come face to face with the one who has wronged you or the one you have wronged. My sense tells me that our churches and homes are like deserts, drying from the lack of genuine relationships, longing for fresh showers of apologies and forgiveness. Will you be the first one in your circle to make a difference? I pray you will.

Why are we asked to apologize to the ones whom we have wronged? Well, the Bible has not used the word "apologize." But there are several usages of the word "reconcile", which means to make one, to bring into unity again. Jesus desires that His family will be in unity. And apologizing brings unity. Further, in very clear words, Jesus spoke to us, as recorded by Matthew:

> ***"If another believer sins against you, go privately and point out the fault…." Matthew 18:15***

> ***"So if you are standing before the altar in the Temple, offering a sacrifice to God, and you suddenly remember that someone has something against you, leave your sacrifice there beside the altar. Go and be reconciled to that person. Then come and offer your sacrifice to God." Matthew 5:23, 24***

The prayer of Jesus recorded in the book of John calls for unity or oneness. Listen to the language:

> ***"...so that they will be united …. so that they may be one, as we are." John 17:11, 22***

I am suggesting that this unity of which Jesus spoke and desired for His family is also obtained by apologizing when we have wronged one another. So why do we apologize? Because Jesus has asked this of us.

We desire to apologize in order to liberate ourselves from the spiritual and emotional bondage in which we find ourselves. When there are distorted relationships between us and others, we are bound. This can cause us to withdraw from church, or home. We resent the sight of an individual with whom we are at odds, therefore we stay away. And staying away makes us losers. I have known individuals who chose to sit on the opposite side of the church in order to avoid someone with whom there was a strained relationship. Others cannot sit in the same church, even though the church is large. Some individuals have become physically sick. Their emotions are too much wrapped around the one who has done them wrong.

Diet, sleep and social interactions have been affected. It seems that their world is suddenly reduced to a peep hole.

We desire to apologize in order that God can increase His presence and Holy Spirit in our churches and homes. God wants to be present where His children are. But when His children are disconnected from one another, and there is no unity, then there is no longing for His presence. And the church or the home goes on limping with its disconnected joints. There are many statements unfolding how God feels about the church and its unity. Here is just one:

> *"The Spirit of God will not abide where there is disunion and contention among believers in the truth. Even if these feelings are unexpressed, they take possession of the heart, and drive out the peace and love that should characterize the Christian church."* Testimonies for the Church, vol. 4, p. 221.

We desire to apologize as an evidence of caring love for the family. We care so much we cannot afford to be separated. We cannot afford to send her to sleep with a painful heart. We cannot afford to watch her walk through the door with tears dripping down her cheeks. There are so many individuals who wander through life as in a maze, puzzled about relationships and longing to make them better. So many individuals sit at a desk in an office attempting to be joyful, but hurting within and longing to reconcile. Do we not hurt with them? Do we not care so much as to release them from their pain? This is why we apologize to them and seek reconciliation, and re-creation of oneness and friendship. We love so much that we deeply desire to dissolve heart-breaks.

Spouse – You spoke a word that was offensive to your spouse. Maybe it was intended to be offensive or not, but the effect was the same. And you thought that it did not matter what happened, life will go on. Wrong. It does matter for this caused heart burn and maybe tears. And this will trouble your spouse for some time. Is an apology in order?

Parent – It is believed that a parent has all the answers to life and from this position becomes a lord over a child. The child's privileges, growth opportunities are denied, suppressed and treated with dismay. The child feels like a nothing. Is an apology in order?

Child – Your parent is not always right. But God asks you to respect your parent. If in your moment of impatience or misunderstanding you were rude or disrespectful, is an apology in order?

Family – In every family there are misunderstandings that cause hard feelings. Have you experienced this and is there a family member who upset you and you are not feeling good about? Then, is an apology in order?

Employer – You are the boss. You have the authority and you lay down the rules. Do you remember the time when your hand was too heavy and you saw the cold, cloudy shadow sweep over the countenance of your employee? You may have caused hurt and pain and you were too busy to notice and care. This pain may still be remembered in a hurting manner. Is an apology in order?

Employee – Working maybe was stressful and that was why you snapped at your boss and work-mate. You were surprised that you behaved that way. But you did. And you are sorry. Is being sorry enough? No. Do you think an apology is in order?

Friend – Even best friends lose control of things. You were mad at your friend and spoke and did that which was inappropriate that caused pain and tears. Friends don't behave that way. Will it all go away and be forgotten? Maybe not. Is an apology in order?

Neighbor – Just across the fence or street, is a heart that is hurting because of a careless word spoken or deed done. Neighbors do this kind of thing. Conversations and interactions may or may not continue. But usually, the hurt feelings will continue for some time. Is an apology in order?

Other – There are other relationships out there that are hurting. Individuals find it hard to function because of the pain caused by someone. If you are involved, is an apology in order?

By now, the Holy Spirit has been working on us and calling us to come face to face with someone who has been hurting because of us. We are being called. We have the options of writing a letter, using the telephone or meeting face to face. We might not be at peace until we obey the directions of the Lord to go and make it right. So let us rise and go. Someone might be waiting for us to come. The Lord might be preparing a heart to receive us. So while the going may seem a challenge, God has prepared the way. And what happens if we refuse to go? Then we will carry the burden and miss the joy and God will keep reminding us.

I do wonder how many have lived in pain and died carrying the pain from being hurt because they never experienced apologies and forgiveness. There have been several funerals of which I have been a part and heard through the tears words of sorrow. Individuals were hurting because of what they neglected to do while their loved ones were alive. And now their loved ones had died and it was too late. There is no use for apologies in the funeral chapel, nor at the grave site. Handkerchiefs can wipe away tears, but they cannot wipe away that which we neglected during life. So while there is life and consciousness and God is calling us to reconcile with the ones we have wronged or who have wronged us, please let us embark on it this moment before it becomes too late. Even if we find it bitter to approach that person, here is a promise, we will find it sweet at the end. Apologizing is ***Bitter and Sweet***.

Do you know of someone who will not accept your apology? There are individuals who are not ready for apologies. I have experienced that myself. Sometime ago I realized that I wronged a church brother. He was very disturbed and informed me of his distress. I then knew that I was wrong and proceeded to apologize. I was very sincere because I cared about this brother. But my sincerity was rejected. He wanted nothing to do with me. Some time later, I again attempted to reconcile, but was rejected. In fact, my gestures seemed annoying to him. What then must I do? Well, I still cared much for him. I prayed and desired the best for him. The Lord gave me a loving heart for him and a peace within. But I knew that he was not ready for reconciliation. Therefore, I allowed him space and time.

There might be individuals you know who are hostile towards you. They want you out of their lives. Then stay out of their lives. Or they want more time to process what happened between you and them. Then give them that time. Though we must show our regrets, we are not to offer our apologies to the ones we know will be irritated by them or who are not emotionally ready. Apologize when apologies are appropriate. You be the judge.

We would wish that our apologies would be received with warmth so we might experience the sweetness that can follow. Realistically, there might be one individual who will reject our apologies as I experienced. It is painful when we are rejected after all our efforts. But rejection does not mean it is time for retaliation or flight. Rejection may mean this is an opportunity to provide more time and love. For more love leads to more determination, more determination leads to more strength, more strength leads to more victory, more victory leads us to become more like Jesus. This rejection, taken in the Christian spirit, will lead us to greater heights, where otherwise we would not have been. This rejection is painful but praise the Lord for it if it makes us better individuals.

What are we to do when someone calls us and desires to meet with us because an apology needs to be made? We may question why, or we may already know what happened. Our reaction may be anger, and we have no time for apologies. So we may need a cooling down time. Or we may just prefer to have that person out of our lives. We may not feel the need for an apology, but the one offering the apology may have been held in slavery by some wrong done and may want to be liberated. To free those people, why not try to give a listening ear with an understanding heart and accept that apology and offer our own if needed? So please create an environment and listen to the apology. Sympathize with the one apologizing. Encourage the person to open his heart. At a time like this, the hurting one often needs to open the locked-away emotions, for these emotions may have been stored for a long time. Based upon what we are told, it may not be necessary for us to contribute to the discussion. A two-way discussion may not be the call of the moment. It is more important to just listen. When the party has concluded opening his heart to us, let us accept the apology and express appreciation for it. There is no need to express surprise or to register that we were long waiting for this to happen. This is not the time for scolding an opened, broken heart. Let us do all we can to create a welcome atmosphere. Let the person know that we warmly accepted the apology and that we freely forgive him. What a moment we have just created. God has been there. God has won again. Friendship has been re-established, and life is again a colorful place desirable for human habitation. This is only true because we received an apology, the outflow from a broken, hurting heart. And what is left for us and that individual is sweetness.

What does apologizing do for me? It makes me humble. It makes me examine the reason for apologizing. It softens me. It makes me more sensitive and I desire less to hurt anyone. It makes me feel free and connected to Jesus. I have also observed that it softens the person to whom I am offering the apology and opens the doors for dialogue and friendship. It is good. It is sweet.

Mere apologies are like band-aids. Band-aids simply cover the wound and do not heal it. This means that when I have caused someone to hurt, even though I have apologized, the hurt is still there. This hurt may last for a short or long time, depending on the personality of the person being hurt and the nature of the offense. For myself and several people I know, hurts usually linger for a while. And at times, only Jesus can remove this hurt. And for that we will praise His name.

Since hurt tends to have such depth and permanence, should we not be more careful about how we relate to others? Oh yes, we definitely should. It is for this reason that I am pleading with my Christian family to do more than having daily Bible readings and devotions, observing the health laws and speaking of the soon coming of Jesus. Please, I am pleading that we accompany these truths with a passion for healthy Christian relationships. Let us study, pray, fast and discipline ourselves to think and examine our ways before we hand them to others. A simple summary: to think before we act or speak. Let our words and actions be seasoned with gentleness, tenderness and Godliness. It is my sense that it is easier to avoid a spill than to clean it up. So let us agree to care more deeply for others, do less apologizing by doing more right deeds and speaking more tender words. This is what Jesus is doing. This is what I want to do. How about you?

Pass me by with the dish of indifference,
but increase my distribution of forgiveness.

Reflection Page

- Has anyone who did you wrong returned to apologize and if yes, how did you feel after the apology?

- Can you think of someone whom you have wronged and it would be good for you to apologize?

- Is it possible that mental and spiritual illness may be caused by unresolved conflicts?

- The Bible records that when one has done wrong he should make it right. What does this mean to you?

- Apologize! Apologize! How does it cause you to feel?

Chapter 10

Simple Steps to Solve a Conflict

I am optimistic about my church. For God is changing people, even me.

Surely, when people share the same space, there will be conflicts. A conflict by itself is not disastrous. The disaster comes when we handle the conflict poorly. In my experience we have not done well in resolving conflict. It seems more comfortable to ignore it by pretending that it does not exist or by doing nothing about it. We the people, even Christians, live our lives hurting and isolating ourselves from our community because of unresolved conflicts. I am sure many have lived their whole lives without the delight of resolving a conflict. On the other hand, some of us desire to resolve a conflict but are very much afraid or do not know how.

If you are one of those who are afraid to face and resolve a conflict, I am creating this section just for you. Please know that this section will graduate you from talking about people to talking to people. The steps are simple and, if tried, they will work for you. They have worked for me. They are my friends. And I wish I had had them many years ago as an active part of my life.

Conflict is natural and realistic. It may seem to be destructive, but in reality it can be delightful. Conflict has the ability to bring individuals together and foster friendships where there might have been misunderstandings and hard feelings. Sometime in my past, a co-worker and I had some struggles. We were misunderstanding each other. When we became aware of what was happening between us, we began to talk and work through the issues. Our minds were opened to each other and our working relationship was improved. From this experience I am able to suggest that the following be tried when there is misunderstanding or conflict:

- Take time to listen and understand.
- Try to see things the other person's way.
- Realize that you are not always right.
- It is not as important to be right as it is important to get along.
- Ask questions for clarification.
- Indicate how you feel and how you see things.
- Give enough time to deal with the issue and person until there is resolution.
- Think of the other person's feelings.
- Feel for what the other is attempting to reach or touch.
- Position yourself to help that person reach her goal.
- Recognize that you cannot change the other person.
- Be willing to change your attitude.
- Understand that we are all humans and be forgiving.
- Pray for the person and the process.

Because conflict seems to cause pain, we tend to run from it. However, when we run, we lose. And while I am encouraging us to stay with the conflict until there is resolution, I am also encouraging us to evaluate and determine which conflicts deserve our time and energies. There are many trees in the forest, but not all bear fruit. And we are in the fruit collection business. There might be several conflicts surrounding us, but there might be little benefit from trying to resolve some of them. Also, there might not be enough resources and time to deal with all of them. Solve those that will bear fruit.

Now, let me introduce to you my niece who is a teacher in one of our Christian Academies. Rodelyn teaches 1st and 2nd grades. Presently, at the time of this writing, she is working on her graduate degree through Grand Canyon University. Through her study she has captured some tools for solving problems without violence. These tools give students the freedom to solve problems by themselves. Students are helped to see another person's point of view and understand how the other person feels. So in her classroom she teaches her students six steps to solving problems. Rodelyn told me about this teaching tool and also wrote about it for her school paper. I am sharing with you her article as it appeared.

"Teaching first and second grades this year has been a fascinating experience.... We have introduced two new programs that have proved to be very successful. One tackles our ability to resolve conflicts.... Often at this grade level, students have a difficult time working through their interpersonal problems. Tattling is a common result of not knowing how to deal with a disagreement. As teachers we try to encourage problem-solving techniques among our students as a healthy alternative. The 'Problem solving' chart has helped immensely. Whenever students have a conflict between them, I encourage them to pull out the chart. Each student involved in the conflict stands on opposite ends of the chart. There are six steps that they follow before the problem is resolved. Each student takes a turn vocalizing his or her needs and feelings. By the time they reach step 6, there is a resolution.

"Since this problem-solving chart was introduced at the beginning of the school year, I have only twice had to intervene and help students work through a problem. The chart is available to students at all times. We keep it rolled up on a shelf and the students pull it out whenever they need it. It has been wonderful to see the students verbally work out their differences in a non-threatening and non-violent manner."

And now I will list the six steps as they appeared in Rodelyn's article:

"Each participant takes turns vocalizing their needs or feelings while working their way to a resolution:

- **Step 1**: **'I want....'** ('I want you to stop bothering me.' 'I want to play with you.')
- **Step 2**: **'I feel....'** ('I feel mad.' 'I feel sad.')
- **Step 3**: **'The reason I feel __________ is because....'** ('The reason I feel mad is because you won't leave me alone.'

  'The reason I feel sad is because no one will play with me.')
- **Step 4**: **'My understanding of you is....'**

  ('My understanding of you is that you feel sad because I won't play with you.'

  'My understanding of you is that I am bothering you because I keep following you around.')
- **Step 5**: **'Maybe we should....'**

  ('Maybe we should try to get along.' 'Maybe I can play with you for half the recess.')
- **Step 6**: **Students then make a decision** between their choices and agree upon it with a handshake."

I can testify that Rodelyn's conflict resolution method does work among her students. One lunch period I visited her classroom. Clarissa, one of her students, must have had an unpleasant encounter with another student, so she came to Rodelyn and registered her discomfort. Rodelyn asked her if she had attempted to work the problem through with the student. Clarissa said no. Without another word from her, she left and approximately five minutes later, Clarissa returned and said, “Mrs. Miner, the problem has been resolved.” And she ran away to play, as if nothing had ever happened. I was startled. I had never before heard anything like this from adults, nor children. But I left the school grounds that day assured that if little Clarissa did this, so can adults.

Let me draw you into a dramatic experience of mine. It is between Lester and me. Lester is a church member in my congregation. Lester is a nice guy and does good things for the church. But Lester often puts out sharp, prickly vibes which irritate others. And no one had the courage to tell him. Does this sound familiar? The time had come for Lester to relocate to another community that would provide him with better opportunities and equipment for his career. Knowing what I did about him and hearing what others had expressed about him, and knowing that his future could be negatively impacted unless he had the opportunity to change, I was challenged. Should I carefront Lester with the concerns about him, or should I trust the Lord to reveal them to him, or let him live his life and reap the consequences?

I knew that the right thing to do was to carefront him, but I was fearful. So one Tuesday night, I went to the Lord in prayer and said, “Lord, if you desire that I carefront Lester about these concerns, please bring him to me and let him ask me, ‘Ewart, what classes may I take to enhance my goals?’” Following that prayer, I rested my case in the hands of the Lord. Two days later, on a Thursday night, a night I am not usually at the church, there I was. As I drove by the entrance, I saw Lester standing by my office door. He saw me and waved at me. We walked into my office together, and I wondered why he was there at that time. So we visited for a short time, and I said silently to the Lord, “If you want me to discuss these concerns, the time is now, for soon Lester will be gone.” Hold your hat, for in the next few seconds, Lester said, “Well Ewart, what classes may I take to enhance my goals?” God worked so quickly that I became momentarily speechless, and I did not know how to respond.

After I composed myself, I shared with Lester how much God loved him and had arranged that very moment. Lester and I spent some time that evening and another evening, as I lovingly shared my concerns with him. We prayed and began to share. We felt the presence of the Holy Spirit. When this Godly moment came to an end, we prayed and hugged. Lester expressed thanks for my courage and gentleness. He said he would be a better person because of our sharing. We left as friends, and we knew that God had won. Could this happen to you? Do you desire for this to happen to you? Would our churches, communities and families be a warmer place if this experience happened there?

It is true that not all situations will have a similar ending. Even if they ended differently, it would have been right to attempt carefronting the brother or sister needing a little loving. So, I am encouraging you to give God a chance to work a miracle, to touch a life and mend a broken heart. As you face your conflict, try the ABC of conflict resolution – four basic, simple steps:

1. **Acknowledge the hurt** – Know that you have been hurt and know the person or persons responsible for your hurt. Be sure your information is correct.

2. **Pray for clarity and wisdom** – Know that it is God's will that you carefront this situation. When you receive the green light from God, then become more intentional in praying for God's will and wisdom. Solicit prayers from others without disclosing the occasion except to those who know of the situation. Establish the time and place of the meeting. Consider a place which will provide comfort and privacy.

3. **Carefront** – Approach the meeting in humility and kindness as God's messenger. Remember that the Holy Spirit is there keeping records of how you treat God's other child. State your concern, your hurt, and how you

treat God's other child. State your concern, your hurt, and how you are feeling. Apologize for any part you may have played in the situation and further offer forgiveness to the person or persons who caused your hurt. Listen carefully to the individual who may want to respond or to clarify. Accept clarifications, apologies and gestures of reconciliation.

4. **Reconcile** – Make clear statements about your sorrow for the past and intention to live in love from then on. Make promises to revisit immediately any further misunderstandings. Make promises to reconcile with any other individuals who might have been affected. Make promises not to allow your relationship to be negatively affected anymore by this situation. Then pray together and perhaps exchange a Christian hug.

There are some occasions where after several days or weeks it may be necessary to ask the individual, "Are we all right, is everything OK between us?" This is just a check–point.

If you desire to be a part of God's miracle, if you desire to set yourself free, if you desire to build a Christian community where people feel free and safe, then please allow God to use you to harmonize His family while here on earth. Avail yourself to God, that He may use you to make a wrong right. Please, if you are willing, ask God to put you to work. Time is short. And as you are now resolving to have God use you, I am experiencing joy because of you. I am proud of you. I am thankful for you. God bless you.

As we attempt to resolve a conflict, expressing how we feel can aid in the process. So let us give thought to how we express our feelings. I am including a few sentences that may reflect how one may feel.

> "At this moment I feel that I am not being understood and this is causing me some discomfort."

"I feel that I am not making myself clear. Ask me some questions about what you think I am trying to say."

"As this conversation continues, I am feeling more and more pressured and uncomfortable, and we are getting nowhere. Can we talk another time?"

"I want to understand you, but something is blocking my mind just now. Please help me to understand you."

"I care about our relationship and I want to work on nurturing it, but right now I am not feeling right about us."

> "Lord, entice my heart and my will to be the reflector of your expectations."

Reflection Page

- Conflict has the ability to bring individuals together and foster relationships. Discuss how this is possible.

- Conflict seems to cause pain. True or false? Is the giver as well as the receiver affected?

- Name a few factors which cause conflicts.

  a.____

  b.____

  c.____

- How have you observed others resolving conflicts?

- How do you usually resolve conflicts?

Chapter 11

Hurting Others

"How beautiful on the mountains are the feet of those who bring good news…."
Isaiah 52:7

Because we are Christians, our relational intentions tend to be good and noble. Deep within ourselves we desire to respect and treat others well. We do not begin the day with a prayer like this, "Dear Lord, lead me today to someone to whom I will express my outrageous anger and derail that person's peace train." No, not at all. It is more likely that our daily prayers are, "Dear Lord, today, make me like You. Help me to help someone in need and to be good to those I meet."

Even with this good prayer and good intention, something happens later and we sometimes touch someone with the touch of death and pain. Something we say or do will hurt a heart. Someone will be discouraged and fragmented. Someone will retire to bed in tears and pain and may fear facing the next day. Someone will be changed for the worse and will be affected for days, weeks, months or even years.

It is true that we may not have intentionally caused the hurt and are deeply sorrowful. Therefore, we apologize, which is the Christian thing to do, but the hurt remains, this is the human nature. A hurting word or behavior is like my escaped balloon. Once on my way to the hospital to visit a church member, I stopped by the store and purchased for her a balloon. In the parking lot, I stepped from the car, reached for the balloon by the string and as it came through the door, it slipped from my fingers and away it went. I stood in the parking lot feeling so useless and foolish, hoping no one was seeing me, for there was nothing I could have done to retrieve the free flying balloon, as it joyfully sailed to nowhere. How I wished that I could have brought it back, but I could never do that. So are hurting words and behaviors. Once said or done, they cannot be recovered, not even by apologies.

****

The Hurters: Who do you think is capable of hurting someone? Only the evil people? I have encountered individuals who have no regard for the feelings of others. To them it does not matter if you are hurt or how you feel. And I wonder if such heartless individuals are somewhere hidden in our churches, or in our homes? I cannot tell your story, but I can tell you mine. I have been hurt by the high level of government in our church, by fellow pastors, and by church members. Well, are not all these Christian people? Yes, they all are. And they claim to have the mind of Christ. And having the mind of Christ, they should have known better. What is sad is that knowing better does not necessarily mean doing better. A church sister once said to me, "As a church, we have much information, but we are not changing." Some intentionally hurt another heart. Others unintentionally.

My fellow Christians, in this book it is my intention to call us to come closer to the heart of Jesus. And there beside Him we will learn the art of loving others with tenderness. Like Jesus, we will aspire to build and not break, to encourage and not weaken, to bring laughter and not pain. I am appealing to us to each day commit ourselves to guard the feelings of others and if, by accident, we slip and cause someone to hurt, hurry and take steps towards reconciliation.

How do we hurt others? We hurt others by what we say to them and by what we say to others about them. There are other occasions when we hurt others by what we do or not do. I will now share a few examples of how we do cause pain. The names used are fictitious, and the situations might be slightly altered to protect the individuals. .

I never can forget working in a large government office complex where hundreds of individuals worked. During my short time there, I had seen a gentleman driving a shabby old car to work. I had particularly noted him because his car drew me to him. What I did not realize was that others were also drawn to this man because of the condition of his car. One day as I was walking by one of the offices, I heard two ladies talking about this gentleman. One wanted to describe him. The one making the description did not use his name. No, she described him this way, "The man driving that old car." I knew exactly who she was describing. Too bad I associated this man with his old car. And apparently, others did also. Isn't it amazing how we recognize the dirt, rather than the daisy in someone?

Sometimes we admire and think the best of others until this relationship is soured by what someone says. One day, Janet offered me some cherries from her tree. She and I picked the cherries. They were delightful, so I ate and ate, enjoyed and enjoyed and even suggested that Janet should supply me with more. Later she told me that among her supply of cherries, she discovered worms. This meant that my delightful encounter with these cherries might have been flavored with worms. Oh, this couldn't be true. And the few remaining cherries were instantly disposed of with agony. My cherries were delightful, until I was told of some of their unpleasant characteristics.

Does this happen in our relationships with people? Certainly. There might be someone in your world, that the Lord has brought there to help you and you accept this person as the gift from God. And sometime later, some dear friend will visit with you to inform you of the poor judgment that person had exercised sometime in the past, and consequently, your relationship with that person might change and the Lord's purpose might be marred. I am not speaking against constructive information. But I am speaking against destructive information that is inflammatory. I am speaking against church members' passion for sharing gossip. Do you know of any one who has been hurt because a church member felt it was his duty to share some harmful information? Have you personally been hurt because of this? Are you one who may have slipped and spoken more than the Lord desired of you?

If you are that person who has caused another heart to hurt, intentionally or unintentionally, and if you have not sincerely cared for that hurt, the good news is that there may still be time to make peace and soothe a hurting heart. But of equal importance is our opportunity to take a different course as we relate to others. By the help of Jesus, we can uphold and encourage them. We can give them direction. We do not have to hurt them, and we should not, especially those of our Christian family. Paul said to his Christian friends:

> ***"Don't use foul or abusive language. Let everything you say be good and helpful, so that your words will be an encouragement to those who hear them. Ephesians 4:29.***

He also said this:

> ***"Whenever we have the opportunity, we should do good to everyone, especially to our Christian brothers and sisters." Galatians 6:10.***

Have you ever wondered why we hurt others? Surely there are multiple reasons. It is my intention to share from my experience, eight reasons.

1. ***We hurt others – When we are angry***

   Barbara Livesay once said to me, "Hurting people hurt other people." When the mind is controlled by anger, the senses seem to be disorganized and rationality is thrown out the window. It is at this time that behaviors tend to be out of control. Our words and actions tend to misrepresent who we really are. It is at this time that we do things which we later regret. And these behaviors do cause hurt.

> *So what should we do when anger has come upon us?*
>
> *Pray, cool down, exercise, take time out, change scenery, shower and change clothes.*

2. ***We hurt others – When there is a misunderstanding***

   When one is focused in one direction, it is easy to miss what another is saying or intending to say. And unfortunately, what is heard is usually the wrong and less desirable thing. The reaction is to respond in kind. This usually hurts.

> *So what should we do when there is a misunderstanding?*
>
> *Clarify, and resolve to be kind and tender, regardless of how we feel.*

3. ***We hurt others – When we are tired***

   We may be physically or mentally tired. When we are tired, we tend to function at a lower level. We are more easily provoked and bothered. And at such times, our words and actions tend to get out of control. Whoever crosses our path is subject to our wrath and consequently will inherit pain and hurt.

So what should we do when we are tired?

Rest, concentrate on our behavior, be kind and tender, regardless of what is said.

4. ***We hurt others - When we are ill***

No one enjoys being sick. Sickness brings with it multiple, complex feelings. There are times when sickness even has the doctors puzzled. They have no sure answers. Well, how does this cause the sick person to feel – miserable, tired, fearful, hopeless, and angry? This anger seeks for an outlet, and if you fall into the space of this sick person and say the wrong thing, you will soon become the recipient of an outrageous anger treatment.

So what should we do when we are ill?

Keep calm, express how we feel, know that others love us and pray for patience.

5. ***We hurt others - When we are rushed***

Many of us are in a rush trying to get somewhere on time. During rush times, listening and concentration are at their minimum because the focus is, "Get there on time." There is no time for discussion or clarification and consequently, the rushing person gives rushed answers, without much thought. These answers or comments may cause pain.

So what should we do when we are rushed?

Be aware of being rushed and soften our answers. If possible, slow down. Make arrangements to continue the discussion later. Be polite and nice.

6. ***We hurt others – When we are jealous***

It is true that God has given each one different gifts. Each one uses these gifts differently, and this is fine. However, somewhere within the human frame is the tendency to compare our different gifts and identify who seems successful or not. If you are more successful than I am, I may resent you rather than rejoice with you. This resentment may make me less appreciative of you and your companionship. And if I am not very careful in guarding my feelings, I may reflect my resentment or coldness to you by the careless, hurting words I throw at you.

So what should we do when we are jealous?

Appreciate our own accomplishments as gifts from God, designed just for us. (In God's mind, His gifts are not better or worse, they are different for different individuals.)

7. ***We hurt others – When we are troubled***

Everyone deals with a measure of conflict which causes the mind to be troubled. These conflicts emerge from various sources and tend to aggravate our lives. And how well do we deal with aggravation? Most of us do poorly. In the times of aggravation, seemingly, the whole body chemistry is thrown off balance into a whirlwind and thinking is not necessarily straight and rational. At this time in life, we are best left alone for a while, for we can be dangerous. This is the time when we may hurt others by our words or behaviors, even without intending to do so.

So what should we do when we are troubled?

Deal with just one thing at a time. Avoid transferring our troubles to others.

8. ***We hurt others – When we are straying***

   Jesus is the principal reason for our peace. When Jesus is present in our lives, the world around us seems to be peaceful. And the manner in which we deal with people reflects the spirit of Jesus. On the other hand, when we are straying from Him and He is far away from us, our behavior tends to be strained and cold. This is when we become careless and hurtful in dealing with others.

So what should we do when we are straying?

Come back and stay close to Jesus. Treat each child of His with Christ-like care.

I cannot believe that any human being has walked the planet without hurting someone. We do hurt people intentionally or unintentionally. Hurts are painful and may result in strange behaviors. When we hurt someone, we may become sorrowful and even apologize, but as I have said elsewhere, apologies do not erase the damage done. This fact is beautifully illustrated in this e-mail someone sent to me.

NAIL IN THE FENCE

"There once was a little girl who had a bad temper. Her mother gave her a bag of nails and told her that every time she lost her temper, she must hammer a nail into the back of the fence. The first day the girl had driven 37 nails into the fence. Over the next few weeks, as she learned to control her anger, the number of nails hammered daily gradually dwindled down.

She discovered it was easier to hold her temper than to drive those nails into the fence. Finally the day came when the girl didn't lose her temper at all. She told her mother about it and the mother suggested that the girl now pull out one nail for each day that she was able to hold her temper. The days passed and the young girl was finally able to tell her mother that all the nails were gone. The mother took her daughter by the hand and led her to the fence. She said, 'You have done well, my daughter, but look at the holes in the fence. The fence will never be the same. When you say things in anger, they leave a scar just like this one.' You can put a knife in a person and draw it out. It won't matter how many times you say 'I'm sorry,' the wound is still there. A verbal wound is as bad as a physical one."

So, it is my prayer and may it be your prayer, that Jesus will season our thoughts and hearts with His sweet gentle demeanor and that our words and dealings with others will be hurt free. Truly, this is not natural or easy, but with Jesus working with us, all things are possible. We can bring joy and hope to others, rather than pain and hurt.

Lord, please share with me a little piece of you,
And let me spread your quality to those around me.
Let me ease the shattered traveler,
And let me feed him with sweet pleasantries.
Let me take pain and hurt away
And let me give hope and joy.

Reflection Page

- Why are Christians not exempted from hurting someone?

- Who is capable of causing pain?

- Do you know anything about church member's gossip and is there anything you can do?

- When do you tend to let your guard down which may cause you to hurt someone with your words?

Chapter 12

Hurting the Hurting

A heart is a tender flower
Tend it with care.

Hurting the Hurting is a subject matter that brings me hurt because it talks about me. And as we expose this subject, you too may realize that it is also about you. You may be the person who had experienced hurt or you may have been the one responsible for engineering hurt. What I hope to examine in this section is how we carelessly deal with someone who is already hurting.

Many years ago, I left my birth home, Jamaica, for a foreign land, Canada. It was my intention to attend college to prepare myself to become a pastor. I had a dream to attend school, but soon realized that I lacked the financial resources. I knew very few individuals in Canada who could help me financially. I courageously approached two of them for help but they offered no help at all. I worked as hard as I could to support myself but soon ran out of funds.

Coming into my second year of college, I was elected to serve as the president of a Seminar Group. You see, I had been active in this group during the previous school year. I had looked forward to serving this group as president and traveling with it preaching, singing and telling others about Jesus and school life. Soon after school started, a school administrator informed me that because of my insufficient funds and my inability to register as a full time student, I could not be the president of this Seminar Group.

The problem was that the administrator knew that I was somewhat embarrassed and hesitant to inform the Seminar Group of my status and that I would need to resign. He did not encourage me to resign or to tell the group. Instead, he volunteered to be present at the next meeting of the Seminar Group to tell them himself. On that Friday evening after vespers, he was there and did just what he promised. It was cold and hurting. Looking back, I would have been less hurt if he had kindly and firmly encouraged me to tell the group myself. This would not have added so many more hurt to my hurting. He never cared about how I was feeling. Maybe he was too dedicated to doing his job right.

****

Bobby is a member of our church. He has always earned the highest respect of the church family and the community in which he held leadership positions. What no one knew was that Bobby was an alcoholic. One weekend, he was out drinking, and on his way home that Saturday night, he was involved in a car accident. His and the other car were seriously damaged. This accident received wide news coverage. Surely the church family now knew that Bobby had been drinking and all marveled at this. Bobby went through his time with the legal system and made the appropriate payment for his behavior. Now, was Bobby sorry and embarrassed? Surely. Was Bobby hurting emotionally because of this? Surely. But he continued to be present for church, hoping that the church family would forgive and accept him. And yes, he was forgiven and accepted. Praise God. Then one day following the church service, a church sister met him and said, "Bobby, I hope you haven't been drinking lately." This was a stabbing dagger to Bobby's heart. Was he not already hurting? Why then this?

Why add to his hurt by reminding him of his past poor judgment?

****

Sally and Jim had been happily married for fifteen years. Together they significantly contributed to their church and every one knew that. Somehow, something went wrong and Jim and Sally found their marriage struggling. Jim talked to several individuals in the church family about his and Sally's relationship hoping to find help. He also sought help from family counselors. But all the help was fruitless because Sally refused to cooperate. She refused to listen to anyone who was willing to advise her about their relationship. Eventually, Sally, working against the counsel of several church members, forcefully displaced Jim from her life and their home. O yes, this displeased the church family and became the talk of the church. Jim took his possessions and left town to start another life. Sally continued to attend her church, but her church family was sure to remind her that she had run her husband away.

Sally found this reminder very hurting and thought that her memories of the event brought her enough hurt that she needed no more from the church members. She even hated meeting the church members for fear that someone would mention that Jim had left because of her. Sally most specifically remembers a conversation that occurred several years after Jim had left in which a church sister asked, "Where has Jim been since you ran him away?" And Sally's heart sank again. Tell me, was this question kind or cruel?

****

Benny and I had spent much time together. One could say we were friends but not the closest of friends. He knew of the things that were important to me because we often talked about important matters. He knew that one of my passions was to be in college studying to become a pastor. He also knew the reason I was not enrolled in college was that there was a balance owing to the school. He should have known that not being enrolled in college for financial reasons and having an unpaid balance caused me some pain. One day, he and I were in conversation and I suppose I made a comment which touched a negative button in him. He became somewhat disturbed. His response to me was very surprising, "When you are able to take care of your school bill, then you can talk to me about my problems." How shocking and painful this was to me. For you see, we were not discussing anything relating to my school bills. Neither had I intended to make him uncomfortable. So why then did Benny choose to remind me that I had unpaid school bills? Surely, his reminder was not appreciated and it just added more pain.

****

Helen knew that her body was not functioning normally, so she went to see her family doctor. He examined her and ordered some tests. After waiting a few days, Helen's phone rang. It was her doctor. He wanted her in his office the next day. There in his office, her tears began to fall because she understood why her body was not functioning well. She had cancer. Do you know how it feels to find yourself in the doctor's office being given this news? Helen was hurting and in tears as she returned home from the doctor's office. The one thing that possessed her thoughts was "cancer." Can you imagine the pain she felt as she told her family and friends of the news? And by now, the only other news she wanted to hear was the news which would bring cheer to her heart.

Helen's church family had heard about her cancer. The church members became sad after hearing the news and had prayed for her. She was encouraged by the way the church family cared for her. But one thing that was not forgotten was that Helen had not functioned in her church office as well as others did. Some felt that she should not be reinstated because of her failure to meet the ultimate mark. But had anyone thought of how Helen would feel if removed from her church responsibility? Had anyone thought of the timing? Yes, it was thought of, but the church felt it was more important that the job be done well. And so, Helen was removed from the one church position she held and enjoyed doing. Some may say, it was done to protect her from stress. But the truth was, more stress was caused by removing the position from her. Can you see that during Helen's sickness she needed to be involved and felt that she was valuable? And rather than encouraging her by involving her, her church isolated her. Helen was hurting on account of the news from her doctor – she had cancer. To add to this, her church family removed from her that which meant much to her, her church office.

****

Shirley went shopping for her much needed bookcase. She found one that was very pleasing to her eyes. Arriving home, she anxiously opened the box and began to assemble the book case. The pictures of the bookcase assured her that she would be able to complete the project within a short period of time. But the pictures were wrong. The project was much more complicated than she had anticipated. After spending several hours assembling, she finally thought that she saw the dawn of day, the end of the project. But then she discovered that there were four significant pieces not yet assembled. And in order to include these four pieces, she would be required to disassemble portions of the already assembled project. This would be a painful task.

She was distressed and mad at herself for missing these four pieces. Just then, her sister walked into the house, into a distressed atmosphere. "What is the matter?" she asked. And Shirley informed her that four pieces were missed. To this her sister responded, "Do you not know what directions are for?" Shirley was silent. Shirley was mad. The last thing Shirley needed was to be reminded of her mistake. Her sister did not need to "rub it in." What would have been appropriate was for Shirley's sister to have said: "I am very sorry. Is there anything that I can do to help?"

****

When one is hurting, one does not need any further hurt inflicted. I do realize that some individuals find it easy to respond without considering the impact of what is said or done. Some of us speak the first words which come to our lips. My plea is that we will give serious thoughts to our words and to evaluate the impact our words will have on the hearer. And if we refuse to contemplate our words and their impact, then we are better off not speaking at all. I am continuing to appeal to us, to think about and stay away from behaviors that may cause God's children pain.

There are many conditions in this life that produce pain and hurt. But please, let us not be contributors to the Hurt Industry. Let us lift the broken heart. Let us comfort and encourage the hurting. Let us dispel pain and implant hope and happiness. It is said: "When one is down, keep him down." But I am saying, "When one is down, lift him up. When one is up, keep him up."

Often we may find ourselves guilty of doing the following:

- Accusing one who has just returned from the doctor with bad news,
- Embarrassing one who has just lost someone dear by death,
- Blaming one who has just failed a test,
- Accusing one who has just received a second speeding ticket in a month,
- Ridiculing one who has just arrived home from a very hard day at work,
- Firing an employee whose father has just died,
- Reminding one of her faults, of which she is very much aware,
- Asking questions that we know will resurrect painful memories.

Sometimes such painful behavior is accidental while other times it is very intentional. Have you ever wondered, "How could a Christian intentionally walk the path to hurt another Christian?" We sometimes hear it said,: "I can't take anymore." This means that there has been insult upon insult, pain upon pain, hurt upon hurt. It has also been said, "We shoot the wounded." This means that when we see one who is already hurting, we inflict more hurt. I am pleading with us to become more caring in how we deal with those who are already hurting. They may be hurting because of their poor judgment. This is true. And when they fall in our paths, is it not our Christian privilege to heal the broken hearts and dry the pouring tears? Some Christians travel with a whip. Others travel with wiping towel. What does Jesus travel with? Matthew has helped me to understand how Jesus cares about the hurting, in these words:

> ***"He will not crush those who are weak, or quench the smallest hope." Matthew 12:20.***

Paul also speaks to how we are to care for the ones who have missed the Christian's mark:

> ***"Dear brothers and sisters, if another Christian is overcome by some sin, you who are godly should gently and humbly help that person back onto the right path." Galatians 6:1.***

My question to you is, how will you care for your Christian brother or sister the next time that person has fallen out of line? Will you extend the whip, to chastise the already hurting person? Or will you apply the warm wiping towel to heal the broken heart and dry the dripping tears?

> Did the Holy Spirit awaken any thoughts in you as you read this chapter? If yes, what and will you share these thoughts with a friend?

Reflection Page

- Have you been hurting when someone added more hurt? If yes, describe how you felt.

- "The truth hurts." – How do you handle this?

- How do you overcome hurt?

- What do you suppose the hurting person desires?

Chapter 13

Hurting the Ones We Love

Where the tears have scorched, plant flowers.

This section is hard to write. It is hard because it is very painful to me. It reminds me of the times when I was careless and my behavior or words caused my family pain. But I must write about it in the hope that I will better relate to those whom I love and that you may glean something that may make a difference in your relationships.

The ones we love may be family or ones we are close to. These individuals are a part of our lives because they are special to us. In the case of family members, we are one. We are part of each other. When one hurts, all hurt. In the case of church members, work mates, neighbors or other relationships, these individuals have come into our lives because of some special common interests that bond us together. We enjoy being together, and whenever one hurts, all hurt. When one is happy, all are happy. The ones we love are the ones we pray for, support and encourage. We will travel for miles to bring them happiness and success. The ones we love are those who feel special because we make them feel special.

When I think about who I am, I know that I would never intentionally hurt the ones I love. But there were times when I was careless and spoke words that caused hurt. Those words were most likely spoken while I was hurrying, tired, angry or just insensitive. But on the other hand, there is no excuse for such behavior. I am ashamed and sorry. But I am learning to do better. This is possible by the presence of the Holy Spirit in me and by my making a conscious effort to be mature in this area. No, I do not expect perfection, but I desire to grow and become better. And when I fall, I expect to recognize what went wrong, pick myself up, apologize and continue my journey, growing.

I wrote earlier that this section is hard to write. This is so because of the emotions it generates in me. You see, when I think of this subject, I think of disappointments. Let me explain. The ones we love expect to find in us love, care, trust and honesty. When these are absent, there is disappointment, brokenness, hurt and tears. You might have heard it said, "I didn't expect this from him." "I never thought she would do this to me. We were getting along so well." Have you ever been hurt by the ones you loved? Or have you ever hurt the ones you loved?

In this life, while we work and live among others, we will most likely experience disappointment and hurt. For some reason, we find it easier to deal with the hurts that are inflicted by strangers or individuals not emotionally connected to us. We let these hurts fall off our backs. Even if they linger for a while, they may soon disappear, leaving little damage. On the other hand, when hurt is caused by the ones we love and depend upon, this digs deep into our beings, wrenches and damages our emotions and may hurt for a long, long time. Some say this damage is irreparable. Others will say this is repairable only because of Jesus living in them. Please give attention to this: **When we hurt the ones we love, it really HURTS.**

"We can hurt them the worst because we know them the best."
Janet Williams

> Lord, please make me gentle and kind. Cultivate in me the appetite to see others as your children and my friends.

So why do we hurt the ones we love? I will attempt to share with you from my personal experience and from what I have learned from others.

We hurt the ones we love because – we know them well.

When we have spent considerable time with an individual, we understand that individual quite well. We know what pleases or displeases him. We know how to push his buttons. And so in times of disagreement, we consider this time right to irritate or hurt that person. When Lester and his wife, Lesmine, had a disagreement, she chose not to come home immediately following work, but went to see her girlfriend and spent several hours before going home. Lester was hurt by this. Therefore, he refused to clean the dishes in the sink. He knew that his wife became very distressed whenever she came home to a sink full of dirty dishes. Notice that both Lester and Lesmine knew what it took to provoke and hurt each other. Would it not have been nice if Lester, though disappointed with his wife's behavior, had cared enough to do the dishes? I wonder how she would have felt when she arrived home and found the kitchen and sink clean.

We hurt the ones we love because – they will understand.

I recall facilitating a Family Life group. In this group, one husband said he was less careful when talking to his wife, because she understood him. Whenever he was talking to his boss, he was very careful because his boss paid him to work and he was protecting his job. This husband thought that he could talk to his wife without caring about her feelings because she would forgive him, she would understand his mood and what was happening in his life. It is true that his wife understood him. But it is false to think that his wife had no feelings and he could treat her any old way. It may be true that we understand, but it may still hurt.

We hurt the ones we love because – they will not fight back.

Some individuals prey on the feeble and weak or those who choose to be submissive and non-combatant. Within some relationships, some of us think that we are bigger, better or have something others do not have. It might be gender, stature, finances, education or something else. And we exercise our false superiority to intimidate or embarrass others. When we speak, all other voices must be silent. This may be more prevalent between parents and children, husbands and wives, employer and employee.

Some of us find personal delight in controlling others. We claim that we are the boss. And what does the boss do? He lays down the rules and expects them to be obeyed without resistance. Unfortunately, some do submit themselves to this condition and just hurt and hurt and almost never complain nor seek for a way out. Some have been under this condition for so long that they accept this as a way of life and refuse to fight back. And so the abuse and hurt continue. Often, the one who supposedly cannot fight back and is hurting is the one who needs love, attention and support. Why then should any one hurt this person?

We hurt the ones we love because – we do not respect them.

We are not expected to agree with everything someone says and does. Each one is given a space within which to operate according to what is right for that person. We are all entitled to see things differently. And all of us can be right, though different. How is this possible? Let me try to explain. Many years ago, working as a printer, I created a picture on a piece of cardboard using a paint brush and several colors of paint. With the paint brush, I just made numerous meaningless strokes, leaving a piece of modern art. If you looked at this picture, you might see nothing. Another person might see a body of water and another, a tree. I saw a picture that looked like my oldest brother. Notice, we may all see different objects in the picture. And who was wrong or right? All were right. The challenge that we face is to be able to appreciate or respect each other, even though we see things differently.

When we neither appreciate nor respect the differences in each other, we may pressure, manipulate or intimidate others to agree with our ways. We want others to think and behave as we do. And this causes hurt. It is so nice to be close to someone who accepts us for whom we are.

How do we hurt the ones we love?

We hurt the ones we love when we make jokes about them. I was seated in the passenger seat while my daughter, U-Lee, did her practice driving. The road was narrow and she passed a mail box, I thought, too close for comfort. So when we arrived home that morning and the question was asked, "How did she do?" I humored the moment by saying that she almost took home a mailbox. For some time, my family used this "Mailbox" humor whenever the discussion was around her driving. The time had finally come for her to take her driving test, and so I thought I would take her for a drive to make sure she was ready for the test. I had prepared some driving instructions and attached them to a clipboard, just as the real guys do. As she sat waiting for me, I approached her and again humored her with the mailbox, and she stormed from the room in tears. At that moment I learned that she hurt whenever we joked about her driving and the mailbox. I had never known that all these years. She could have told us, but that is not the point. The point is, we had been hurting her all this time and did not know. We had been hurting the one we loved. What we thought was humor was painful.

We hurt the ones we love when we make jokes about them in the presence of friends. Lesmine had been married to Lester for several years. They had a wonderful family and things were going well for them. One day she approached me and informed me that she was planning to separate from Lester. She was tired of his jokes about her when they are with friends.

He got his kicks at her expense. She was very embarrassed, cried inwardly and would take this no longer. This is interesting, for many of us are guilty of making jokes about others and everyone seems to get a good laugh. Even the ones being joked about will laugh outwardly but are hurting inwardly. So the next time you are at a party and feel like making the moment happy by telling jokes, please be careful. Do not hurt the ones you love.

I came across another story about family relations. I am including it here for you.

FAMILY

"I ran into a stranger as he passed by,
'Oh excuse me please' was my reply.
He said, 'Please excuse me too;
I wasn't watching for you.'
We were very polite, this stranger and I.
We went on our way and we said good-bye.
But at home a different story is told,
how we treat our loved ones, young and old.
Later that day, cooking the evening meal,
my son stood beside me very still.
When I turned, I nearly knocked him down.
'Move out of the way,' I said with a frown.
He walked away, his little heart broken.
I didn't realize how harshly I'd spoken.
While I lay awake in bed,
God's still small voice came to me and said,
'While dealing with a stranger,
common courtesy you use,
but the family you love, you seem to abuse.
Go and look on the kitchen floor,
you'll find some flowers there by the door.
Those are the flowers he brought for you.
He picked them himself: pink, yellow and blue.
He stood very quietly not to spoil the surprise,
you never saw the tears that filled his little eyes.'
By this time, I felt very small,

and now my tears began to fall.
I quietly went and knelt by his bed;
'Wake up, little one, wake up,' I said.
'Are these the flowers you picked for me?'
He smiled, 'I found 'em, out by the tree.
I picked 'em because they're pretty like you.
I knew you'd like 'em, especially the blue.'
I said, 'Son, I'm very sorry for the way I acted today
I shouldn't have yelled at you that way.'
He said, 'Oh, Mom, that's okay.
I love you anyway.'
I said, 'Son, I love you too,
and I do like the flowers, especially the blue.'"

FAMILY – Are you aware that if we died tomorrow, the company that we are working for could easily replace us in a matter of days? But the family we left behind will feel the loss for the rest of their lives. And come to think of it, we pour ourselves more into work than into our own family, an unwise investment indeed don't you think?

A Prayer for Us:

Lord, make me a builder of people
Especially the ones I love
For they are yours
And they are a part of me
Take every hurt from me
Replace in me Your tenderness
Refresh me with Your graciousness
And let me bring with me your joy.

"We can hurt them the worst
because we know them the best."
Janet Williams

Reflection Page

- Discuss this statement – "The ones we love expect to find in us, love and care, trust and honesty." What happens when these are absent?

- Discuss this statement – "We can hurt them the worst because we know them the best."

- What should be done by the one who is hurt?

- What affects you more – the pain inflicted by the one you love or by the one less important?

- Are you easily offended?

Chapter 14

I Have Been Hurt – What Do I Do?

Lord teach me to spread soft, sweet, smelling petals where there is a broken vase.

*Y*es, I have been hurt by church members, family members and friends. So have you. People have done things to me knowing that I would be hurt. Others have done things, and I do not know what they were thinking. But I was hurt just as much. When we are hurt, what do we do?

Because we are all different we respond differently to hurt. However, since every reader of this book belongs to the human family, I can guess that our response to hurt is represented by one of the five approaches that I will be presenting to you. I take responsibility for creating some of these responses. Here they are – Confront, Carefront, Beerfront, Bearfront and Nofront.

1. Confront - This is the act of coming face to face with a hostile person in an attempt to make the truth known at any cost. Often when we confront someone, we have reached our limits of patience, we are upset, we want to set the record straight and put an end to this behavior or whatever it is. It is not natural or easy to accomplish all this without the parties breathing some anxieties and hard feelings.

Neither do I know of any incidents when having confronted, the parties are left as dearer friends and looking forward to meeting again. The opposite is more likely. There have not been many times when I was confronted. But the few times have stained my memory forever. The occasion was painful, very painful.

I am now thinking of one situation when a church member confronted me. This person came to me as if I were an enemy and had no feelings. He came to me as if we did not belong to the same Father and share the same goals for the Lord and His church. I tell you, when I was worked over, I felt worthless. For a long time I carried the pain, but praise God for the resurrection experience, because after a time, I came to life again.

Those of us who used the Confrontational approach might have said something like this, "Lester, rumor has it you said that my husband and I are not getting along and are thinking of separating. Did I ever tell you that? Even if we are separating it is none of your business." I assure you that there were no hugging and warm wishes at the end of this confrontation. Can you recall any occasion when you were confronted? How did it feel? Have you had the need to confront someone and how did you do? Would you do the same again if the need arose?

Confrontation is usually painful. Since we, the possessions of the Lord, may be so fragile, we shatter like glass when confronted. When we find it necessary to set the records straight, let us carefully consider the other person's feelings before we use this Confrontational approach.

> ***"A gentle answer turns away wrath, but harsh words stir up anger….Gentle words bring life and health…." Proverbs 15:1, 4.***

2. Carefront – This is the act of coming face to face in a spirit of love, clarification and reconciliation with someone who has done you wrong. This is when one comes to show you that you are loved, even though there might be a disagreement and she longs to understand you better so as to minimize further misunderstandings. This is when one comes to you and tells you the truth, or bad news, in such a manner that you may even feel respected, appreciated and good.

Those of us who have used the Carefrontational approach might have said something like this, "Lester, there is something that has been bothering me. I heard that you were talking about my family. Can we get together and talk about it? I know we can work this out and still remain close friends." Or maybe it is a bit more involved. "Lester, I wanted us to come together because we have been friends for a long time and have respected each other dearly. Something has been bothering me for some time, and you might be able to help me settle this. It came to my attention that in a conversation, you made reference to my family, specifically my husband and me. Do you recall that conversation? Somehow that information has distressed me, especially since your name was associated with it. In fact, I am still hurting because of this. But I do not want this to affect our friendship, so that is why I wanted us to talk and clear up any misunderstanding. Lester, is there anything that you want to ask me or tell me so that I might get a better handle on this situation and build our relationship?"

Usually, after a meeting like this, the parties feel good about each other. Friendship is restored and the future seems brighter. The parties have a better understanding and a clearer plan about how to deal with each other. This is the approach that builds a family, friendship and a community.

3. Beerfront – This is the act of coming face to face in a spirit of recklessness and carelessness as if intoxicated by alcohol. I have heard it said that if you want to tell someone what's on your mind, just get drunk and you can say anything. It is true, I have observed this done. Now, please note that I am not advocating in any way the use of alcoholic beverages. This is simply a reference, to show how alcohol influences one's behavior. It may allow you to conduct yourself in different ways than if you had not consumed it. The Beerfront approach has no regard for one's feelings. Words are used that tear emotions apart. Individuals are called mean names, which embarrass and humiliate. Accusations are used which have no truth and make no sense. But one thing is sure, the accused is hurt.

The one who chooses this approach may say something like this, "You are so lazy and good for nothing. You are always sitting around. The only thing you do is watch that dumb TV. Dinner is never ready when I come home, and if it is ever ready, it is either burnt or half cooked. When are you ever going to get going and find a job so that I don't have to work so hard? Look at the kids, they have nothing to wear or eat. I ain't talking to you about this again." When one examines the language in this scenario, one will discover that the accusations are false. But the accuser wanted to cause hurt and pain. And he was successful.

4. Bearfront – This is the act of coming face to face with someone who has done you wrong with a spirit of destruction, to gnaw that person like a bear. Bears usually are not friendly and catch our attention as objects of destruction. The Bearfront approach is used when the delivering party knows that the receiving party is weak and fragile. It is also used by the party who professes to be strong. But all that this approach wants to accomplish is destruction. It does not care about how it affects and who it affects. It does not even care about how God feels or how the church or family will be affected. The Bearfront approach meets you face to face and tells you straight. It will tell you the truth plus more. And when the work is done, you are emotionally destroyed. And who cares? In fact, this is what is desired for you, to become spiritually, emotionally, and socially dead.

My sense tells me that the Bearfront approach likes to work in the company of others. It likes to have witnesses, for the more witnesses there are, the more the celebration at the emotional graveside. This approach rips us to shreds like the claws of a bear, and there is very little left. Only the palms of Jesus can rescue us from this cruel approach and make us whole.

Who tends to use this Bearfront approach? Some would expect me to say the ones who use this approach are those who have no knowledge of God, do not read the Bible and do not attend church. But you and I know differently from experience. We know that the ones who have used this approach are individuals who have sat beside us in church, those in whom we have confided our trust, those who sit in high places in church organizations, those who profess to be our friends, and who talk and smile with us. And we wonder, "How could this be?"

Leah and Lorna were church sisters and best of friends. Naturally, they did everything together and exchanged secrets. But what Lorna did not know was that Leah was sharing confidential information about her with the pastor. Not only did she betray the trust put in her by sharing confidential information, but it was intended to be destructive and would hurt Lorna. Leah knew very well that this information would hurt and destroy Lorna. Then why did she do this? I cannot understand, since they were friends. In fact, this information did hurt and destroy Lorna. The result was disastrous not only for Lorna, but for the church.

Sometimes, Christians gather at board meetings or business meetings to execute the Bearfront approach. At these times, there is no thought given to the value of a soul. We do not think of what God has done or could do for this poor struggling soul. The church is bent on silencing that person. It wants to do what is right because the book says so. This is the Bearfront approach.

5. Nofront – This is taking the position to do nothing and say nothing after hearing that someone had done you wrong, even though you are hurting. This may be comfortable for some and difficult for others. Some are of the personality and temperament who want to come face to face with opposition, while others walk away from it. There is a place and time for both approaches.

The Nofront approach encourages one to do nothing when accosted. Let us look at the life of Jesus. He was falsely accused and had good reasons to defend His cause, yet, He remained silent.

> ***"He was oppressed and treated harshly, yet he never said a word. He was led as a lamb to the slaughter. And as a sheep is silent before the shearers, he did not open his mouth." Isaiah 53:7.***
>
> ***He did not retaliate when he was insulted. When he suffered, he did not threaten to get even. He left his case in the hands of God…." 1 Peter 2:23.***

The other day, I called my brother who lives in Jamaica just to say hello. Soon in the conversation it became clear that he had something to say, something of importance. As he continued, my temperature was rising. So I hastened to conclude the conversation before a fire broke out. Actually, there was an emotional fire. I then turned to Lynn and remarked, "I will never call him again." As I stewed and foamed, I thought that my brother needed to know that his words to me were unacceptable and hurting. I was hurt, and felt he should never do this again. But what would this do to him? This would hurt him, and now two people would be hurt. Is it better to have two hurt than one?

Then I resolved to grow up and bathe my hurt with understanding, forgiveness and tenderness. You know what? A few days later I called him to wish him a Happy Birthday. He is my brother and I love him. And he was swollen with joy at my call. And I was no longer hurting. This is how I dealt with my brother. Would I have done the same to one of my church family? The Bible suggests that the church family is comprised of brothers and sisters. How nice it would be if we cared for each other as I cared for my brother.

There were several occasions when others had hurt me and there was an energy burst to respond. But when I counted the cost and the reason why I was hurt, the Lord led me to place the individuals and circumstances in His hands. He would care for them.

So, I have been hurt, now what do I do? I may use any of the above approaches: Confront, Carefront, Beerfront, Bearfront or Nofront. Truly, it is my desire to use the Carefront approach or occasionally the Nofront approach. There might be times when I will be tempted to use the other approaches, but my Christian heart, hopefully, will call me to the most caring and peace – making approach. It is my desire to treat others who have hurt me, as I desire to be treated. I will love them with tenderness in the way I deal with them. This means that when they hurt me with words or deeds, I will, by the grace of God, go and reason with them. This is the Carefront approach. But before I go, I will want to spend time in quietness with God seeking His love, words and wisdom.

I must also add that I need to pray to God to strengthen me and give me wisdom that I will not be broken by every passing wind and therefore I will not need to Carefront every hurting event. If, every time I have been hurt, I find myself knocking at someone's door, there will not be enough time left for sharing the gospel of Jesus.

Then there are some of us who are very easily hurt. Someone blinks at us and we are hurt. We are so self driven and tender that others have to be very careful when they are around us. Granted, we have the right to hurt, but not to make others feel guilty by suggesting that their behaviors offended us. There is a limit to this. We are to learn as we grow, to process what is happening around us, give attention to what is valuable for growth and discard the others. There are times when we need to be tough, strong and not pushed by every little wind.

No one desires to be hurt. But when one is hurting this may be an opportunity to grow, seek wisdom and develop Christ-likeness. How we deal with the hurt and the one who caused it will tell the world about the "stuff that we are made of." Are we strong, understanding, compassionate, forgiving and Christ-like? The next time someone hurts us, remember that Jesus cares about how we respond. Remember that our personal growth and the life of the person who caused the hurt hinge on our response. Our tender loving response can make a difference. Here is a word picture of how Jesus dealt with people, written by Ellen G. White in the book, Steps to Christ, under the chapter, 'God's Love for Man':

> *"He was never rude, never needlessly spoke a severe word, never gave needless pain to a sensitive soul. He did not censure human weakness. He spoke the truth, but always in love. He denounced hypocrisy, unbelief, and iniquity; but tears were in His voice as He uttered His scathing rebukes."*

And again from the wise man:

> ***"A gentle answer turns away wrath, but harsh words stir up anger… Gentle words bring life and health…." Proverbs 15:1, 4.***

"Different doesn't mean wrong."
Gary Parks

Reflection Page

- Of the five approaches which ones do you think are most frequently used?

- How do you usually respond when you have been hurt?

- How can you use a hurting situation to cause growth?

- Discuss the following-

  "He (Jesus) was never rude, never needlessly spoke a severe word, never gave needless pain to a sensitive soul…. He spoke the truth, but always in love."

Chapter 15

The Gardener

When there is a brook
in the back yard, why
walk for miles
to draw water?

Gardening is one of my hobbies. I know what it takes to work with plants and flowers. I handle them with care and they usually are fruitful. However my discussion in this chapter is not about plants and flowers but about people dealing with conflicts. It is my observation that people dealing with conflicts, like flowers and plants, appreciate Tender Loving Care. So the remainder of my thoughts in this chapter will deal with the individual who delivers this Tender Loving Care as a peacemaker between people in conflict. I see his approach to be like that of a gardener, therefore I name him ***The Gardener.***

The Bible addresses how a conflict may be resolved. Let us view two examples: Jesus said if there is a conflict between two they are to attempt to resolve it themselves. If they are unable then involve one or two others. (Matthew 18:15-18). Paul said if there is a dispute between two people do not take it to the secular court, but instead bring it to the Christian family. The Christian will someday judge angels and therefore are quite capable of dealing with human concerns (1 Corinthians 6:1-6). In these two examples we see that God believes in using the human agent for conflict resolution. This encourages us to use capable individuals available to us.

These individuals are usually sought for at distant counseling centers when we may have them available right in our midst. Rarely have I ever thought that a ***Gardener*** who has the natural gifts of a mediator for resolving conflicts can be found in our local church or place of employment. There may be others as well who can be trained for this. Why not use them? The focus of this section is to encourage the use of the capable individuals among us as ***Gardeners***.

In a recent conversation with a friend, she told me that her church for the first time has considered having a "Mediator" who would be available to assist in resolving conflicts among church members. I affirmed her church for this for I had never previously heard of this happening. Hearing this encouraged me even more to write this section.

The church community is well acquainted with the word "discipleship" which means training to become like another or to become a follower. We train individuals to utilize their God-given gifts to become Bible workers, health instructors, greeters and so forth. Why not identify and use those with the gift of gardening. In every community there are individuals who can do the work if given the opportunity and direction. When we have found them let us disciple them and encourage them to help bring people into harmony. As the Bible indicates these ***Gardeners*** are within our church family:

> ***"To one person the Spirit gives the ability to give wise advice…. Here is a list of some of the members that God has placed in the body of Christ:… those who can help others, those who can get others to work together,…." 1 Corinthians 12:8, 28.***

So let us look among us, especially in church settings, for ***Gardeners***.

Why are we to use the capable individuals among us? It has been my observation that humanity tends to gravitate to the familiar. Many will have their cars serviced by the mechanic who is known to them or shop at the store where the owner is a local boy. This means that the ***Gardener*** among us who is known and loved might be a wise choice to help resolve conflicts. The people may share their hearts with him because they know and trust him. They know that he has their best interest at heart.

A ***Gardener*** may not always have the right answers but he is always a genuine caring person. I must hasten to add here that a ***Gardener*** is not a counselor. He should not conduct himself as one and he should make this clear to those with whom he works. The ***Gardener*** is simply a genuine caring person who is interested in helping others resolve their conflicts and assist in building a healthy, peaceful community.

At this time you may be looking at your community and wondering whom among you is qualified to become a ***Gardener***. Without attempting a complete list of qualifying attributes let me suggest seven which I think may work:

1. ***Caring*** – When Lesmine has a concern and is seeking help, she will be looking for someone who cares about her and what is happening in her life. She will want to hear caring words and a caring voice. She will want to see caring body language. What Lesmine appreciates more is knowing that someone cares. When she knows this she will go to great lengths with him. She may place her concerns and even her very life into his hands.

2. ***Mediator*** – Often, the person who comes to the ***Gardener*** is distressed about a situation with someone. This problem has caused a rift in their relationship. One or both desire a solution. This situation may require a peace maker. There may be times the ***Gardener*** must point out bad behaviors that make the situation worse in order to allow the people to recognize their part in the conflict. But, his main objective is to attempt to bring

the individuals into harmony. The ***Gardener*** is not the one to decide justice or a settlement. When fighting individuals are brought into harmony, they may determine what justice is or may choose not to pursue it. While justice may not build a community, harmony and peace may.

3. ***Trust Worthy*** – It is my sense that when one has a concern, one wants to share this with someone that is trustworthy. This person is easy to talk to and will protect confidential information. Personal information will be shared with only those previously agreed upon. In my case, the person whom I trust is the one to whom I will tell those things which are dear to my heart. Sometimes, when I am troubled, right answers are not what I am looking for. I just want to talk to someone who will understand me and keep my secrets. This is a noble saying, "I can tell him anything. I can trust him with my whole life."

4. ***Good Listener*** – Good listeners are rare. Many of us do very well on the talking side and talking is a good quality, but at the appropriate times. As a ***Gardener*** the ability to listen is paramount. This listening does not only mean being silent. It means being attentive and interested. Sometimes there is the tendency to listen in order to give the right advice. If that is the only reason we are listening this may cause us to lose the point being made. A good listener hears what is being said and asks the appropriate questions to draw out what was not clear. It is so nice to hear the other person say, "You helped me express my feelings exactly." Sometimes a troubled heart may not be crying for right answers, instead it may desire a heart to which to pour its burdens, and a heart which is willing to listen. Good listening also involves the ability to ask questions for clarification.

5. ***Non Judgmental*** – It is easy and natural to predetermine who or what is right and the motives for certain behaviors. Our personal experiences help us to do this. If we see someone sitting beside the road begging we think he's a bum. But often the truth is different from our assumption. In the not too distant past, someone had done me wrong and I was upset. Later, he sent me a gift. Rather than joyfully accepting it, I tried to find reasons why it was given and my thoughts were not necessarily good. Fortunately, I caught and scolded myself for pre-judging his motives. Since I did not know the motive behind the gift, I should have accepted it joyfully and attached to it only good intentions.

   The other day I telephoned a friend and he promised to return my call that evening. Evening came and went, as did the next day, and there was no call. I began to wonder if our friendship was slipping and should I even call again. I decided to call and was relieved by his welcome voice. He said, "I am so glad you called because I had lost your number." It is essential for ***Gardeners*** to be open minded, accepting, and gather all the information. Then and only then can one have a better view of the situation. Avoid jumping to conclusions without knowing the facts.

6. ***Not Taking Sides*** – Taking sides means favoring one over the other. Parents often are drawn into situations where they are tempted to favor one child over another. They deal with complaints which tend to make one child the bad guy while the other is good. This is the explicit purpose of the complaint. Those of us parents, who take time to do what is fair, tend to not fall for the "who's right or who's wrong game."

   We listen to the concerns of the children and attempt to lead them to see the other person's point of view and encourage them to cooperate with each other. We know that the better response is to be neutral.

   Taking sides may create more conflicts. One

person may appreciate us, while the other may not and they may eventually resent each other. We will want to resist the temptation to identify one as wrong and the other right. So as we attempt to mediate the concerns of others, our focus ought to be, unity.

7. ***Prays For Wisdom*** – The human mind and behavior are very complex. Often they are beyond our comprehension. I personally do not believe that there is any text book with all the answers which will fit every person dealing with conflicts. Everyone will need to be listened to and nurtured differently. How does one know the appropriate answer or direction to give? This is when the ***Gardener*** calls upon God for wisdom.

   Please do not think that we call for God's wisdom only when the situation is challenging. No. Calling for God's wisdom is what needs to happen every time we are dealing with people. Seek His wisdom at the beginning and at the end thank Him for being with you during the session. Also, let us keep this thought close to us – During the session, if there seems to be immovable tension, pause and invite each one to take time to seek God's wisdom. A praying ***Gardener*** is connected and tends to be successful.

I hope that these seven qualifying attributes will be helpful. They have worked for me whenever I used them. Please remember that this list is not complete and neither are the thoughts under each attribute. Add others from other sources or from your own experience. Use what works.

In which settings are we to place these ***Gardeners***? Place them wherever there are people and conflicts. ***Gardeners*** may serve in the church family, the community, school, home, work place or elsewhere. Surely their functions will differ based upon the location. But the idea of having someone local to facilitate harmony is worth using everywhere.

Let me now share five benefits of using ***Gardeners***:

1. **Replace Court System -** The Bible makes it plain, (1 Corinthians 6:1-6) that Christians are not to take their concerns to the secular courts but to other Christians. So having ***Gardeners*** will help to keep us out of the courts.
2. **Using Natural Gifts -** Developing a ***Gardener***, is recognizing and encouraging someone's natural gift. There are so many individuals who have natural gifts which are not recognized. And their worth goes unnoticed and is wasted.
3. **Personal Growth** – This is an opportunity for the ***Gardener*** to improve his gift. As he works with individuals his skills as a ***Gardener*** will become sharpened.
4. **Familiar Environment** – Having a ***Gardener*** on site may convey to others that someone cares. And it might be consoling to be able to talk to one with whom we work or fellowship.
5. **Share Privilege** – As a pastor, I am expected to resolve church members' conflicts. I have spent many pleasant, productive hours on this. But had I thought of the idea of ***Gardeners***, I would have involved them in the ministry of conflict resolution and hopefully they would have enjoyed and grown in this area.

Some are presently using ***Gardeners***. There might be others who have never thought of this idea. I am encouraging them to give this more thought. This idea, if put into practice, may make a difference. One may never know the full value of this until it is tried.

One will never know the taste of a fruit, until it is eaten.

Reflection Page

- If you are dealing with an unresolved conflict, to whom are you inclined to disclose it, one whom you know or a stranger?

- What are the strengths and weaknesses of having local ***Gardeners***?

  Strength________________________________

  Strength________________________________

  Weakness_______________________________

  Weakness_______________________________

- What other attributes would you like a ***Gardener*** to have?

  a.______________________________________

  b.______________________________________

  c.______________________________________

- If you were asked to become a ***Gardener***, would you accept, and why?

Chapter 16

Love Me with Tender Words

Lord, invigorate our intentions.

Words are used daily. Everyone living and conscious uses words. They are used as means of communication. Words have an immeasurable impact. They give life or cause death. They promise a future or condemn one to failure. Words do much more than this moment can portray. Damage may be caused by many words, few words, or even just one word. So often we throw out our words carelessly, not giving thought how they may affect someone.

Since words can do so much, is it not appropriate that a few moments be dedicated to them? The wise man of Bible history once said:

> ***"The words of the godly lead to life…."***
> ***Proverbs 10:11***

> ***"Gentle words bring life and health…."***
> ***Proverbs 15:4***

> ***"Kind words are like honey – sweet to the soul and healthy for the body." Proverbs 16:24***

The following are quotations from different books and authors dealing with words:

Webster's New World Dictionary of Quotable Definitions, arranged by Eugene E. Brussell

"Words are what hold society together." Stuart Chase

"The dress of thoughts; which should no more be presented in rags, tatters, and dirt, than your person should." Lord Chesterfield

"The most powerful drug used by mankind."
Rudyard Kipling

"Words are loaded pistols." Jean-Paul Sartre

Mac's Giant Book of Quips & Quotes – E.C. McKenzie

"Let all your words be kind – nobody resents them."

"Remember, there has never been an overproduction of kind words."

"Never part without loving words. They may be your last."

"Kind words do not wear out the tongue – so speak them."

"Words and feathers are easily scattered, but not easily gathered up."

Shakespeare once said:

"These words are razors to my wounded heart."

Alfred Lord Tennyson once wrote:

"Man's word is God in man."

Words – are our friends or they may be our enemies. They are life or death. They make or break. As I write and reflect on the power of words – I feel the need to be so careful about my words. It is my prayer that my words will be enlightening and encouraging. I desire that my words will cause others to feel that they are valuable and important. And when in conversation others will feel good during and after. I would so much love my words to be touched by God. How about you? For our words to minister life and encouragement to others, the Holy Spirit must be our daily partner, seasoning our thoughts and words.

Can you remember the times when you were discouraged and low and someone called you or a member of your family came to you and spoke words of comfort, hope and encouragement saying?

> "I have sensed that for the past few days you have been dealing with some hard issues. I just wanted you to know that I have been thinking of you dearly and praying for you. You will make it all right. And I will be right here for you, regardless."

These are the words that bring healing, health and happiness. These are the words we love to receive in the good or bad times.

As you reflect on these few thoughts about "Words," think about the words you speak to your family members, work-mates or friends. Are they healing, encouraging words, or cutting, destructive words? Do you have reason to regret or rejoice having used them?

> "Lord, make me to see others as your tender creation.
> No, they are not perfect and all beautiful
> But you love them.
> And they have hearts that hurt and laugh.
> Lord, make my lips pure and delightful.
> So they may feel the tenderness and love of you."

Reflection Page

- Identify a time when words negatively affected you.

- Identify a time when words positively affected you.

- Note an occasion when your words had a negative or positive affect.

  a.____

  b.____

  c.____

- How many healing, encouraging words have you spoken in recent times, and what were the occasions?

- What would happen if our prayers included a request for words that are positive and encouraging?

Chapter 17

To You with Love

God's greatest gift is,
LOVE
Accept it.
Share it.

*I*n these troubled times, people are especially longing for a love that is tender and true. People are yearning for a love that is patient, kind, warm and understanding. The pace of life is swift and the torrents are swelling over our heads. The hearts of mankind are lonely and are failing. I can hear the bellowing and I can see the tumbling as stormy faces search for a place of calm and love. I can hear the laughter and I can see the sunshine as love clasps hands with turmoil, as we reach out and love someone for Jesus.

To you, I extend my plea with love, that you will join me and the Christian family to spread petals of tender love to every one whom God sends to us. There is no greater gift that humans can share than the gift of love. God is calling us to possess a little piece of His heart. He wants us to display His character and splendor. He wants to make us agents of peace, beauty and love. This is God's offering to me and - ***To You, with Love***.

As we live a little longer here on this troubled earth, we will continue to walk among people. Where there are people, there will be differences and strained relationships. This is one of the facts of this life. But my plea is that we will not focus on the differences and the strained relationships. Rather, let us by God's help see people as God's gold. Let us concentrate on the gold. Let us see the challenging person as the one, wonderfully made and loved by God. God placed that person in my path for me to love and grow with. And God is counting on me to be faithful. God gives us opportunities that we may grow. He gives these individuals to me and - ***To You, with Love***.

What do I do when Lester and I cannot see eye to eye? Do I just walk away? I may, but no one wins. No one gains anything. No one grows. Recently, I have been learning from life's realities, that when iron rubs against iron, there is the possibility of a shine coming through. Therefore, I must stay with Lester though he is difficult to live with. Thus we can work out the difficulties until we see a shine coming through. Then the Lord will have won and so will we. We are to intentionally pray and work for the persons who challenge us and who are different from us. We are to entertain pleasant thoughts about them and keep wishing for good things to happen to them. When you are struggling with an individual, please do not walk away and hide even though it seems easy to do. Instead, intentionally pray for that person, speak pleasant words about that person, and one day God will open an opportunity for you and that person to have a better working understanding and appreciation for each other and you may even become buddies.

Recently, I was encouraged when a church member spoke of me as being a friend. We were not always friends. We have had rough times. We worked out our differences and we never gave up on each other because there was gold in both of us. Thanks to God for opening our eyes to see the gold. Some people readily display the gold. Others take raking and digging. But if we are patient, we will see the gold, for God placed it there and He wants us to find it. God gives this challenge to me and – ***To You, with Love***.

Sometimes, strained relationships weigh heavily on us and we would love to unload them. It is at these times we need the heart of God. It is at these times we need to understand the compassion and staying power of our God. It is at these times we need to remember that God sees us as special individuals and has a passion to be one with us. Our God does not unload us because we are difficult. My belief is that as we understand God and appreciate Him for who He is to us and we desire to come close to Him, we will want to share the same with others, even the difficult person. Have you ever thought of praying for the person who does not talk to you? Have you sought for opportunities to talk wonderfully about the person who speaks mean things about you? Would you even intentionally sit in the same pew with the person who disdains you? Do you desire to love that person just like Jesus loves her?

It is not natural or easy to love the unlovely. But it is the God-like thing to do. Praise God, He loves me just as I used to be, as I am and for what I can be. I admire my God for this. This God is teaching me how to love the one who does not love me and who is difficult. It is not easy, but I am growing. It actually feels good to overcome bitterness and to love the one who caused the bitterness. It feels good to be free from self imprisonment, caused by holding resentment against someone. It really feels good to be free. This freedom is from our God to me and - ***To You with Love***.

> "Please give me the language and touch of reconciliation.
>
> Unite the kingdom of your people through me."

Now, if you and a church member are not on speaking terms, or it might be a neighbor or workmate, or classmate, what would your God want you to do? Are you sensing that I am calling you to own a little piece of God's heart, a heart that is bent on love, unity and reconciliation? You are right. I am appealing - **To You with Love**, to pray for wisdom and strength to reach out of your comfort zone to the person or persons with whom you have strained relationships. Work the works that will make smooth the rough paths. Rub the rubs that will diminish the rust so that the shine can come through. And bear the pain that comes from laboring in love. Let us go and tell that brother, sister, spouse, parent, child, friend, neighbor, whoever, that we are sorry and that we are asking for forgiveness and Love.

"Lester, the other day, I did you wrong by________. I should not have done that to you. I am very sorry and I promise not to do that again. Will you please forgive me? Will you please give me a chance to love you? And we can be friends."

I would like to dedicate the following love lines firstly to my wife, Lynn, secondly to my daughter and son U-Lee and Ewan, and then to all those whom the Lord has attached close to my heart:

God loves me,
And I love you,
I dream of you,
And you are worth my tears.

Your name is in my heart,
Because you are dear,
Have no fear I am with you.

Speak to me about love,
Speak to me about fear,
I will hear you.
I will care for you.
We are running behind in time,
But take all the time you want,
I will be waiting for you smiling.

Walk the path of life,
Fall the fall of life,
And I will catch you at the bottom.

Smile at me,
Laugh with me,
We will sing together in the storm.

I believe in you,
You are God's treasure,
My time is yours in pain or joy.

Your presence is a garden,
Your kindness is sunshine,
Fruits are growing all over you and me.

Yesterday is gone,
Tomorrow is uncertain,
But today I have you and that matters.
God knows you,
God knows me,
And God puts us together, forever.

My friend –
Take a moment to cultivate love,
Take a moment to listen to love,
Take a moment to experience love,
Take a moment to give away a little love,
For what matters is
LOVE.

From me -
To You with Love

Reflection Page

- Have you ever been hurt by someone? What was it that hurt you?

- You and an individual are struggling. Should you walk away? If your answer is no, what are the benefits from staying?

- Is there a correlation between the way we love God and those around us?

- Discuss how much God loves you.

Chapter 18

From My Heart to Yours

God's great gift to us is others. Our great responsibility is to love them.

*H*ad there been a moment in your life when you were troubled because someone had hurt you and the pain still lingers? Has there been a moment in your life when your spirit was low, because there had been a collision between you and a church member, a workmate, a neighbor or family member? If your answer is "Yes," then there is no reason for you to carry this pain any longer. I invite you to identify the source of your pain. (What is your pain?…………...)

Once you have identified the source of your pain, then I further invite you to desire and pray for the opportunity to engage with the one who has hurt you. Bring the troubled past into a refreshing present. Carefront and resolve the conflict. Let God transplant His heart into the heart of the conflict and you will begin to breathe a fresh breath of ease and peace. This is an exciting growth experience.

It is my sense that God smiles when He knows that His children are about to make peace, for He knows of the present and future benefits. He knows of the joy that will flood the mind. He knows of the burden and weight that will be left behind. So, why not put a smile on God's face by carefronting your conflict and breaking the barriers which separate love?

If you at this very moment are involved in an unresolved relationship that continues to aggravate you, I encourage you to take this time to pray for strength, courage and wisdom. Then go forward. Seize this moment. The rewards are too rich to lose. So walk in the company of the Holy Spirit and God. Speak with the grace of Jesus our Lord and the favor of heaven will accompany you and give you peace and love. God bless you.

Once you have experienced this and have felt the touching results, you will want others to experience the same, for good things are for experiencing and sharing. So invite others to celebrate with you. Tell them of how you have been delivered and lightened. Invite them to walk the path you walked to resolve your brokenness. Assure them of your prayers of support as they walk this path. Encourage them to become community builders and love cultivators, by healing broken hearts and breaking down walls which separate.

It takes one bomb to destroy a city.
It takes one sun to light the world.
It takes one person to change a community.
It takes one to make the difference, you.

Now that we have spent this time together, you surely have caught a piece of my heart, and it has been my privilege to have borrowed your time. After all that we have shared together, please know that what I desire most is that we will always say to one another:

Love me
Laugh with me
Care for my feelings
Treat me as if I were you
Teach me that I may grow
Pray for me and pray with me
Make me feel that I am special.

Speak to others nice things about me
Send me sweet thoughts wrapped in rose petals
Surprise me with a card or a happy telephone call
Shop for the little thing that makes me smile.

I will walk great distance for you
I will love and nurture you as a garden
For God planted you beside me
Next to my heart
And I want to be close.

I will stay close to you
I will listen to your heart
Let your tears fall on my face
Let me warm them with my tender love
Let me hear your heart beats for they are music.

I am not asking that I be your best friend
Only give me a piece of your heart and time
And ***Love Me with Tenderness***
And I promise to do the same for you.

Ministries Information

Ewart is committed to support ministries wherever there is a need, with special interest in the countries of: The Philippines, Jamaica and India. The specific areas of ministries are education for youth and the teaching of the gospel of Jesus. Proceeds from the works of Ewart go towards these ministries.

Ewart's works:

•	Love Me With Tenderness	Book	\$10.00
•	A Quiet Place	Devotional Book	\$12.00
•	Sharing A Quiet Place	Musical CD	\$15.00
•	Coming Home	Musical CD	\$15.00
•	Touching Him	Musical CD	\$15.00

(Please add \$3.00 for postage)

To help someone experience the comfort and joy of Jesus, mail your order to:

A Quiet Place Ministry
P.O. Box 511,
Woodburn, OR. 97071

The call of God and the purpose of life are
to love and serve others.